ONE LEG OVER

ALSO BY ROBIN DALTON

Aunts Up the Cross
An Incidental Memoir
Dead is a 4-letter Word
My Relations

Robin Dalton was born in Sydney in 1920. In 1946 she moved to London, where she now lives. She has worked as an intelligence officer for the Thai Government, a literary agent and a film producer. Her first book, a memoir of her childhood, *Aunts Up the Cross*, was first published in 1965 and is now a Text Classic.

ONE LEG OVER

Having fun—mostly—
in peace and war

ROBIN DALTON

TEXT PUBLISHING MELBOURNE AUSTRALIA

textpublishing.com.au

The Text Publishing Company
Swann House
22 William Street
Melbourne Victoria 3000
Australia

First published by The Text Publishing Company, 2017.

Design by Jessica Horrocks.
Typeset by J&M Typesetting.

Cover photograph: Robin with fiancé US pilot Joshua Barnes, from the author's personal collection.
Internal photographs from the author's personal collection.

Printed in Australia by Griffin Press, an Accredited ISO AS/NZS 14001:2004 Environmental Management System printer.

National Library of Australia Cataloguing-in-Publication
Creator: Dalton, Robin, 1920– author.
Title: One leg over : having fun—mostly—in peace and war / by Robin Dalton.
ISBN: 9781925355949 (paperback)
ISBN: 9781925410303 (ebook)
Subjects: Dalton, Robin, 1920–. Celebrities—Biography. Man-woman relationships.

*For my darling grandchildren—Lyndall,
Rory, Carrick and Becan—in the hope
that it will not embarrass them*

FOREWORD

I HAD just written an ebook about death—love seemed the next best thing. I began—it was fun—it ambled from memories of love life to love of life, sex inextricably mingled with 'love and romance, facing the music and dancing', memories of how much I have enjoyed being a woman of my time.

Today, most of the best-selling novels by women writers include, or are dominated by, descriptions of sex. Poor Jane Austen, George Eliot, the Brontes would jostle for place on the list. The four major elements in their stories have shifted in prominence during my long lifetime. Now it is sex; if lucky, love; even luckier, romance; possibly respect—the first squeezing the last almost out of existence, having little relevance to it. How glad I am to have been born at the exact time I was, when the order was (1) romance, (2) love, and (3) if lucky, respect. We did not admit to the relevance of (4) sex. That was slipped in somewhere between romance and love but of course we did not acknowledge that it was the engine which drove them. It hovered in the background and when it leapt to the forefront it was cushioned by the soft haze of preliminary romance, followed by love. Quite often we did not recognise the importance of respect and quite often it was never achieved.

Today, for a large proportion of our society, sex jumps to Number One, and that leaves little room for romance. It might lead to love which in turn might lead to respect, but it seems a pretty bleak progression to me. To the generation before mine, the essential elements to a pairing of the sexes were different again—custom, money, position all coming first. I would choose the order of my era and I look back upon it with nostalgia: 'the way we lived then'.

CHAPTER 1

AT NINETY-FIVE I have begun to dwell on the past rather than an increasingly less intriguing future. The past was a glowing and intermittently rosy place: the future rather murky. No glows on the horizon: thoughts of much loved children and grandchildren cause worry and despair for their world, which appears an abyss rather than the springboard which, in retrospect, was mine.

What, not whom, do I miss most in this nonagenarian reverie? It is being in love. There never was a time when I was not, actively, in love—starting at around six years old with a passion for a gay family friend. Except for the numerous film stars and matinee idols of my youth, I don't remember any of it being unrequited. One floated on a cloud of love affairs, more or less effortlessly gliding from one to another. There is some satisfaction in having lived one's entire life in this delicious state; and what an exalted state in comparison to the lot of many of today's young, who trust the internet rather than a flutter of the heart—sex first, love, if you are lucky—to follow.

We embarked on our teenage years with innocent expectation. We talked to each other. We wrote little notes to each other on actual paper. We met each other at dances and occasionally balls. From the age of twelve, in my precocious case, I could count on at least one 'dance' per week when our parents stayed in the background, turned over their gramophones, relinquished their drawing rooms, parquet floors or verandas to our tentative feet, and we waited to be asked to dance by the boys in their best suits, one or two in white gloves which protected our carefully chosen party frocks from their sweaty palms. Nearly all of us marked up our first kiss from one of these boys, snatched in a corner of a garden or bend of a stairway: all of it the perfect grounding for the years to come as soon as we left school. At the teenage parties, we drank very little alcohol; at least we thought we did. We believed sherry to be the only permissible drink: when asked what one would like my demure response would be 'only a sherry'. Bottles of this lethal drink must have assaulted my young liver, or perhaps lined it as a protection against the heavy drinking in the years to come. When we graduated to later teens we upped our intake in the sophisticated world of cocktail parties, at which alarming concoctions were gulped down our ignorant throats. This may have been good training for the war years, during which we drank whatever we could grab with our ration cards. A miracle indeed that I threw myself into the immediate post-war world of champagne for breakfast with a serviceable liver. It still seems to be functioning.

Later we would meet in what I remember as glamorous dimly lit restaurants, the dance floor surrounded by tables, the band leader of the day perhaps playing 'your tune'. If female and young enough in the 1930s and 40s you didn't really know what an erection was, or meant: it was something encountered on the dance floor or in the back of one's parents' car. Looking back from a lifetime of experience I would say it was more exciting: they don't even touch each other on the dance floor today.

My own good memories continued in that I lived, aged eighteen to twenty-four, through a world at war when the boys and young men we met were all, briefly, on leave, with the unspoken fear that they might never return. Sometimes, when sleepless, I amuse myself with trying to remember those lovers—sometimes taken to bed on a first encounter—counting on both hands in swift rotation; one or two forgotten and having to be slipped in later. I once told this to my friend Diana Athill, who agreed to doing the same and has since made the newspaper headlines by repeating it. But it is not the somewhat irrelevant sexual act I remember. It is the preliminary romantic music as we clasped each other on the dance floor or the deep gaze over a supper table—magic—one was in love. The words of the tunes we danced to were the romantic delights of the 1930s, 40s and

50s—Ray Noble, Cole Porter, Gershwin, on to Hammerstein—
the more serious and long lasting of these love affairs marked
in one's memory as 'our' tunes—'Night and Day', 'Thanks for
the Memory', 'You'll Never Know' (how much I love you), 'You
and the Night and the Music'...The words were like electric
signals between one and the boy of the night: surely he, too,
was thinking that those words were written just for the two of
you—an electronic purveyor of his emotions.

Recently, I noticed a book in my local library entitled
How to Fall in Love. I did not open it but I wondered what the
instructions could possibly have been. Did she (the poor author
a woman) give the advice I would give, although difficult to
achieve on today's dance floors—Just dance 'Cheek to Cheek',
and you may have started on 'The Bumpy Road to Love'. These
were two great tunes.

Now that I have outlived any opportunity for active involvement, the magic power of the old tunes remains. Halfway
through my life Frank Sinatra became a friend and I joined the
list of people to whom each new recording was sent, so I can still
pop his 'Night and Day' into my player and be transported back
to my mother's parquet floor, circling around it in the arms of
Wuzz Stuart, shortly to be killed in the war.

* * *

Almost as much as by the tunes my romantic dreams were
wrapped around the clothes I wore—most of them remembered

as attachments to the arms in which one was currently clasped. In the Sydney of my youth, the procurement of them took up a great deal of teenage time. I was a teenager with my mother's passion for clothes in my genes. Childhood dressing up meant for me ball gowns from her wardrobe. She lost no time in taking me to the top salon in Sydney as soon as I could be got out of school uniform. The most chic and favoured salon was in what we thought was the most glamorous building in town, the St James Building. As for the identity of the salon, the name Rocher, with French pronunciation, keeps urging itself into my brain. The owner was most certainly not French—nor indeed the hinted-at Parisian with which we had mentally labelled her. I am almost sure her name was Fels, and there was a whisper that she was in fact Hungarian.

The dresses I grabbed would be, had I held on to them, worth a fortune today, labelled 'Vintage' and rarefied vintage at that. There was a Vionnet, the legendary Vionnet—pale, shimmering lilac and silver finely pleated lamé, on the finest silk, like a Grecian sheath, with low V neck, sleeveless and simple as a Greek tunic—but, oh, the cut! There was a Schiaparelli tweed two- perhaps three-piece suit. I did not actively like it. The tweed prickled and it was certainly too thick for Australian climes: the colours were Schiap's signature—lilac, purple and 'shocking' pink. (So famous that 'shocking pink' became forever after a standard colour.) There was a little Schiap hat: we never left the house without a hat for any social occasion or even luncheon with a school friend. I now wonder from whence came the money for these lavish luncheons. They were recorded in the Society pages of the newspapers so they were not at some local cafe and I expect Mme Fels was happy to be publicised in this way.

Back to the dresses—Vionnet, Schiaparelli, and Alix! Alix (later to be renamed Gres, or perhaps it was the other way round) was my favourite and as I had a good enough body her softly draped and pleated creations moulded themselves to that body. I remember a dark green fine wool pleated jersey particularly, perhaps because I did not give it away until much later, to my daughter in whose cupboard it may still hang. There was a tight, green, severely cut one in some sort of shiny silk which I can remember because I have a newspaper photograph of myself striding down the street in it (with hat and long white gloves, of course) clasped at the arm by my first young love. Then Maggy Rouff—I have more than one photograph of me in Maggy Rouff—they don't look so good and I do not look back on the only two I vividly remember with affection. This is probably because, in one—a strapless white crepe evening dress—I am photographed with my new fiancé, John Spencer, and in another—a studio portrait—with sequinned top and long pale pink silk skirt, at the announcement of my engagement. Unfortunately, I married the fiancé.

* * *

I would like to have learnt true romance from this first of my three husbands but must substitute my first teenage boyfriend.

We loved each other but our passionate outpourings of love and teenage fumblings never led to full sex. Although the fumblings went a touch too far late one night on the 9th hole of the Collaroy Golf Club, evidenced by a touch of blood on the lining of my taffeta ball dress (subsequently seen by my mother with obvious conclusions reached)…romance filled our days. We met when I was sixteen. He was twenty-one. (I think the episode on the 9th hole happened on my eighteenth birthday.) When I contemplate the many emotional relationships in my life, surely the most romantic suitor was he. Our first kiss took place late at night as he drove me home from our first date. We had stopped by a vast stone wall, on which, the next day, he painted in permanent white paint an appropriately huge heart, an arrow piercing it, and inside it our initials and the date. My initials being identical to those of my father, this may have added to my father's fury as he passed the wall each day on his way to work. The paint took many years to fade, far longer than did our romance. Not, however, before my love stopped a flower seller in the street wheeling a barrow load of violets, my favourite flower—bought both barrow and contents and had them delivered to our door. My doctor father's patients had to negotiate their way past the barrow on their way in and out.

As my young love worked for one of our daily newspapers, he enticed the typesetters to print a poster for display on the street newspaper sellers' boards on the anniversary of this first date, proclaiming the event with our names and the date. This also greeted my father whenever he ventured out. On the eve of that anniversary he enlisted a pianist friend to play, whilst he sang, the tunes to which we had danced all year, ending with 'Thanks for the Memory', recorded on a gramophone record—in those days quite a technical achievement. Shortly thereafter we had a tiff. With wrenching regret, I remember I broke the record over his head. When I last saw him at his ninetieth birthday party, he grabbed me and whispered 'I still love you…I will always love you.'

In some happy pocket of our world, would something similar happen today?

* * *

In my adolescence and in the tight little circle into which I was born, marriage was simply the natural progression from school, rarely university. One fell in love, chose the engagement ring and acquired a vast trousseau of lace trimmed nightdresses and floating negligees (I remember swansdown figured largely), crepe de chine panties, which we called 'scanties' (whatever happened to crepe de chine?) and trunk loads of monogrammed sheets, tray cloths and napkins.

I was eighteen when I met my first husband. He was thirty-one and had just returned from some years in Europe, and was thereby already invested with glamour and romance. He sent my mother flowers every day until I accepted his proposal of marriage, made on the night of our first meeting. During seven months of our engagement, I, too, was swamped with flowers and old-world courtesy. On the eighth month he started drinking and, alarming as this change was, it was not sufficiently so as to induce me to cancel the trousseau, the bridesmaids' dresses, the pink lily of the valley, dyed pink for the cake, in its turn dyed pink to match the pink tulle wedding dress; the pink and white daisies ordered with which to tether the bridesmaids' wrists in a daisy chain—a fancy which struck me as so stunningly original that I could not bear to forgo its execution. It was far too late to stop the nuns in some distant Belgian convent who had been industriously stitching and hemstitching the sheets, napkins, tablecloths, and never-to-be-used tray cloths, for months—each one ostentatiously emblazoned with my soon-to-be-brand-new initials; or to take back the cream hide suitcases, in ever diminishing sizes, the hat boxes and shoe boxes embossed in gold with those same initials, the shower teas—indeed, the church. Nor did I know enough of the world to recognise that what I had chosen was a true, classic, one hundred percent genuine alcoholic. And nasty with it.

From this husband I learnt nothing except the capacity to survive. During the five months' duration (weekends only) of my marriage I did not even learn what an orgasm was. Neither did I learn this from the American servicemen with whom I exultingly tripped through the first years of our Pacific War. It took the British Navy, our second wave of wartime visiting servicemen, to teach me this. All those Americans with so little sexual expertise does sometimes make me wonder about the sex lives of American women of my generation. And if the first husband had been a good lover, might I have put up with the bullying, at least until the novelty had worn off?

The war put paid to both the marriage and the clothes shopping. Even in Australia, in our relative distance from the horrors of Europe, we had our Pacific war, our casualties, our rationing, a bomb or two, a tiny unsuccessful invasion by a Japanese submarine. No bacon because the pigs were shipped to England; little fabric because it was being made into parachutes (nylon stockings unheard of until the Americans arrived bringing with them their p.x. stores); little sleep because we went straight from working at the U.S. supply depots or driving a truck by day to the arms of the pilots or sailors on leave by night. Sydney was the rest-and-recreation base for the U.S. Army services in the Pacific—a short plane ride from the fighting.

Our dancing didn't stop. We scanned the casualty lists for our erstwhile young Australian partners but our new partners, the pilots and the sailors, were on a brief two- or three-day leave from the Pacific skies and oceans, so we fell much more frequently in love, the turnover changing once or twice weekly. What would seem like shocking promiscuity—not only physical but emotional—in peacetime, was felt as a beneficence of the heart. We were in love. The fact that one was rarely caught out in one's perfidious spread of affection blinded one to the dangers. If possible, our affections were limited to one per squadron, or P.T. boat, or Marine battalion: our chief dread was that their leaves would overlap. They seldom did. Enormous pleasure was then to be had from the exchange of passionate love letters, or those which got through the censors and the bombs. I had a fairly standard one to exchange each week, sent to a variety of recipients. I gathered two American fiancés, one engagement ring (still on finger) and was the cause of one divorce. All in the name of love, and romance. Surely more satisfying than the internet and the iphone?

It was great fun to be a woman: we would never have thought of claiming equality of the sexes. We just got on with making the best possible use of our gender, believing it to be a blessing and a bonus, having no desire to compete—rather to ensnare. However brief the romance, we always envisaged marriage as its natural progression: hence the frequent marriage proposals. I don't think we thought further into the future or to the wisdom or suitability of the proposed alliance; the intention was an open door as to how we spent the present.

CHAPTER 2

I REMEMBER, too, exposure to that which is now collectively called the media as being a happier experience than what is to be expected by today's woman. I take no newspapers on a regular basis. I absorb information about the world from a couple of well written weekly periodicals, but at the hairdresser's or in the dentist's waiting room I grab a *HELLO* or an *O.K.* from which I learn about the lives, doings and surroundings of a whole world of strange people of whom I have never previously heard and who are called 'celebrities'. I search in vain for some guide as to their contribution to this society in which they appear to have reached the pinnacle of achievement. I usually fail to find one, although football seems to be an important yardstick, and marriage to one of these husky young men being the key to inclusion in these glossy pages and glittering bowers. But should one of these newsworthy creatures fail to uphold the perfection of their private lives, the media pounce with glee.

Being female is no protection from exposure and public scorn, as it was in my youth. How innocent and naive seem the comments we could expect in the gossip columns of the 1920s, 30s, 40s and 50s. We had not achieved anything either, living a cosy life which must have been privileged if we were deemed interesting enough for inclusion in these columns. It was an indication of our socially blinkered view of the world but it was harmless enough and never was a woman criticised in print. With the spectacular and singular exception of my own divorce, a husband never divorced his wife. For a modest fee, he rented a room in an obscure hotel, hired a strange female, arranged to be discovered in bed with her by the waiter with a breakfast tray, handed over this evidence to a solicitor and gallantly went to the financial gallows as the guilty partner in the subsequent divorce. The wife was able to sail on with her unblemished life. The financial outcome was never reported, neither the eventual share out nor settlement, nor the size of the husband's assets.

My divorce was spectacular and exceptional inasmuch as I knocked the war news (I sometimes boasted that it was Dunkirk but I think it was too early in the war for that—possibly Libya), not only off the front pages but acquired sole prominence on the news sellers' boards with just two words, SOCIETY DIVORCE. My husband, at a distant training camp, was having me followed: I, meanwhile, was having a lovely time, but none of the three co-respondents named in his suit had actually risen to the occasion. In one case, a cup of coffee alone in my apartment late at night, coffee spilt when the detectives burst in; in one there had certainly been romantic embraces, vividly recorded in purple prose in my diary which had unbeknownst to me been read by my husband; the third a day time visit from a portrait painter who wished to paint me. The poor chap who had been sipping the coffee lost a distant mistrustful fiancée who did not believe his innocence because of his gallant offer not to contest the suit; the painter, being Hungarian, had to ask my father the meaning of the word adultery; and the star of my recorded schoolgirl dreams never learnt of his fame, having been an American sailor on a three-day visit to Sydney, now safely back at sea. Not a shred of evidence, but the coffee guest was my only chance on the horizon for freedom from the disastrous marriage if the court case was to be undefended. One could not divorce a serving officer during the war: I would have remained married to a very nasty man, albeit serving the war in nothing more dangerous than a training camp, where he remained. He might have made a fearsome adversary had he got to any fighting front if his five-month chastisement of his teenage bride had been an indication. Those five months consisted of five weekends only when he came home on leave for two days of drunken bullying. I don't remember him actually hitting me but I do remember being forced to throw rubbish on the floor so that he might watch me clean it up, getting into a bath full of dirty laundry so that he might watch me stamp on it, and the gravy running down my face from the first dinner I ever cooked, after it was thrown at me. I was told I was spoilt and like a young horse must be broken in.

I was sent to stay with friends in Melbourne to escape the publicity of my divorce: my parents stayed at home to face it. On a visit to Sydney, decades later, I spent hours in the New South Wales State Library learning all about myself...wonderful stuff, although I hope my writing style has improved: in court my published teenage diary had given Barbara Cartland a run for her money. Nor was John to be outdone in phrase—worthy of Eleanor Glyn was his last remark to me as I fled the apartment: 'I know you have never been unfaithful to me but if I can't have you I'll make sure no one else will ever want you.'

He also ripped off my body all the jewellery he had ever given me. Later, I did manage a midnight raid to recover some wedding presents, and some pieces of my 'dowry' such as the monogrammed sheets, similarly monogrammed cutlery and china, spirited away by my mother and myself from the abandoned marital apartment for which I still had a key. What should be a sad reminder remain in use. Pity about the monograms, which my children are condemned to live with.

I did see my jewellery again. Many years later his second wife called me in London. On the telephone she explained that she wanted to meet me, but she could not come to tea to which I immediately invited her that day as she wished to look her best when we met and that would involve a visit to the hairdresser. The date was set for two days hence.

'I've always longed to meet you,' she said. 'I was so jealous of you when I married John and I said to him, "What was Robin really like?" and he said "She was a dear, sweet, little girl, with the most beautiful legs in the world." And'—with this she reached out and patted one of the legs—'you have!' On the outstretched arm I spotted my wedding ring, my engagement ring, my wedding present diamond ring, my birthday present diamond-and-pearl bracelet, and, looking upwards, my Christmas-present diamond-and-pearl earrings. I wondered if the rings had had to be altered to fit.

She seemed a very nice woman and certainly eager for a chat. 'John was so proud of you, you know,' came next. 'He had albums of photographs of you that he used to pore over; you were like his little daughter he had produced and launched on the world himself.' I murmured, as I poured the tea, that he had had a very strange way of showing his affection.

'Oh well,' came another pat of the hand, 'you hurt his pride you know. You were very immature.'

A sip of tea and a sigh, and then, 'I'd say two things about John as a husband, wouldn't you? He's both ghastly and wonderful—with the accent on the ghastly!'

I would love to meet John Spencer now. I would love to know what his thoughts and emotions were. The poor man was thirty-one when we married and was unprepared for coping with a teenager; if he is to be believed, a spoilt one. He was not particularly good looking. I don't think he was amusing; albeit, being a successful barrister, he must have been intelligent and a good talker. I don't remember what we talked about.

He was not a tremendous performer on the dance floor. Yet, I must have been in that magic state—love—to have married him. I do remember being very impressed that he had been two years in Europe, and by the privacy of his large studio bedroom and bathroom, professionally decorated by the most chic decorator in town, in his mother's beautiful house in Sydney's most desirable location. The colours were navy blue and a somewhat downlifting red we called 'maroon'. I remember this red piping on his navy blue sofa, armchairs and divan bed, on which I lost my virginity, realising that my previous young love had not quite managed it and that I had joined the adult world.

I did lose an opportunity to ask him these questions many years later but was so jolted by a sudden face-to-face meeting that I did not think to grab him as we passed. As I was opening the street door from the Royal Sydney Surf Club on to Bondi Beach, he was coming in. We passed each other in silence.

John Spencer finally died, of drink one assumes, and I only hope his wife continued to have some wonderful moments and also managed to hang on to my jewellery. Sadly, he did not die soon enough to make me a widow in the eyes of the Catholic Church. So, one subsequent Catholic fiancé, Torbert Macdonald, failed to put love before an hysterical mother and the priests; and my dear husband, Emmet, suffered excommunication, a registry office wedding, and death without the solace of religious rites.

By the time my divorce decree became absolute I was twenty-one, in a world at war, and in a part of the world where we experienced all the excitement of a frontline recreation base and few of the dangers. For my twenty-first birthday my father gave me a divorce and a typewriter. The first had cost him a lot of money, and with the second he hoped I might make some of my own.

CHAPTER 3

THE WAR and my father's gift of the typewriter had given me the idea that I might actually work for the visiting young American gods. With such an incentive, I enrolled in a secretarial college and spent three sleepless weeks absorbing the skills on offer; normally a two-year course. It took little more than a chance meeting one night to find my perfect niche. Our American servicemen with whom we danced and flirted nightly had to be fed, clothed and armed: these necessities being supplied by the U.S. Army Services of Supply, based in Sydney. With my new, untested skills, in a brief interview I acquired a job and a boss, the C.O. of this Service. I typed out the orders: soon my boss left the choice of ordering to me. I gained my first experience in the feeding, clothing and bedding of men.

Before the war, girls and young women from the more privileged strata of society did not go out to work. Their goals were engagement and marriage, except for the tiny minority who went to a university. It is generally thought that the lives of women are far better now, but not being of feminist inclination, I am not too sure of this. We did not, in general, enter the masculine workplace: should we be forced, in the absence of the wedding ring, to 'work', our place was either behind a counter as a saleswoman in an upmarket store, or behind a typewriter as a secretary. Such a thing as a 'p.a.' was unknown. By the time the war had ended I had become accustomed to early rising, discipline, and had learnt to type, since proven extremely useful, as well as how to take dictation, swiftly forgotten. The fact that I could work, even earn a living wage, was stored in a comforting mental back pocket, although in what capacity was unclear. I was too busy falling in love to care.

As the focus of the war shifted to the Pacific and Asia, and France was liberated, the American pilots and marines gradually went home. One barely had time to dry tears before the British Navy arrived. There were no more nylons or candy: instead we had cocktails aboard the war ships, the American ships having been 'dry'. My current American fiancé being trapped back home in Boston, I acquired a British one.

His name was John Mackay, not a sailor on one of the ships but a paratrooper in the Lancers, waiting to be dropped into Japan when the atom bomb was dropped instead and the war changed again. He was shipped back to England, closely followed by my next 'trousseau', chiefly new clothes this time, as well as some of the marital recoveries. He was not only beautiful to look at, sterling in character, enchanting in personality, but suitable in every way in my parents' eyes. I had, at last, fallen in love with someone beyond reproach. He was a far, far too nice and decent young man to have been treated as I then treated him, as my passport to England.

I was desperate to get to England, as in Johnny's absence, I had fallen in love again, with one of the naval officers, the young David, Marquis of Milford Haven. My divorce was the main reason we never married: we remained deeply in love for five years, melding into a lifelong friendship. We were never engaged—I was already engaged to Johnny—but we hoped to marry. (I do, however, still have David's ring on a finger.) Because David was young and penniless except for his naval pay, we imagined ourselves in need of family approval and support. In those days (they would not dare suggest it now), any direct descendant of Queen Victoria, as was David, needed to ask the reigning monarch's permission to marry. The Duke of Gloucester was then the Governor General of Australia: David made a tentative approach to him. I was a divorcee. He received a fairly gruff response. We put our plans 'on hold'.

When David left, in command (his first) of the last destroyer to leave Australia, I was determined to follow, and we hoped things would look rosier for us in Britain, to which I was now allowed by my parents to go, ostensibly in order to marry Johnny.

Meanwhile, whilst still in Australia, although officially engaged to Johnny, and unofficially to David, it had never occurred to me to change the habits of the war years. Our nightly haunts, Romano's and Prince's, were still available and although the influx of U.S. and British troops had dried to a trickle, there was still ample opportunity to meet, dance with, and flirt with a constantly changing flow of admirers (such a lovely, old-fashioned word whose usage and meaning have disappeared). Whilst I hung around waiting for the necessary permit to get out of Australia to join Johnny, David, and the trunks en route to Glasgow, I had busied myself with just such an admirer. His name was George Silk, one of the star photographers of *Time-Life*. He was about to be posted to Shanghai, and left days before I did; not before, however, I had tentatively promised to marry him, too. I think Shanghai was the main attraction, and I regret not having at least a trial trip there, the last chance to have seen it in its great days.

CHAPTER 4

IT MIGHT be easier and quicker for women to travel alone today, but we no longer expect help or chivalry (another lovely old word) from men along the way. We join the queues and battle for space with them. They may lift a heavy suitcase from an airline or railway luggage rack if you are lucky but I doubt they will do much more. On this, my first lone travel, I was the first female civilian to get out of Australia, shamefully so privileged because a friend of my father's was the chairman of Qantas. Travel was still restricted by wartime rules: a 'priority' was necessary—no civilian aircraft and no passenger ships.

I was cosseted from start to finish of what in retrospect should have been a terrifying ordeal. I had nothing awaiting me except a charming fiancé in Glasgow whom I unceremoniously dumped as soon as my luggage had arrived, shipped by his regimental army transport, and the true object of my affections and intentions—my young lover, disapproved of by my parents, in London.

My five fellow passengers, in reality middle aged but to me elderly, were men on important government or army missions. The Lancaster bomber in which we started the first leg of the journey was equipped with six hard metal seats facing sideways into the fuselage. I cannot recall how they managed it but somehow they constructed a sort of sling hammock for me to lie on as they crouched, knees to shins, on the chairs below. On every stop along the way my comfort and entertainment were their concern. In Cairo they escorted me to dinner at the then-famous Shepheard's Hotel. At Karachi, in March/April 1946 a city torn apart by the fighting for independence, one of them escorted me to a hotel for the night, protected me for three days from chaotic rioting in the streets and the next day gave up his travel permit to get me on a plane out. He was probably stuck there for weeks, without a permit. In Sicily the remaining five came with me to the market and carried back to England my huge pile of oranges and lemons bought for my waiting, rationed hosts. We were transferred to a Sunderland flying boat; after landing at Southampton, I saw none of them again. I am ashamed at not remembering their names or attempting a feeble thank you. They were men and I was a woman so it seemed normal to me.

We went by train into London, where I was met by Qantas officials and taken to a hotel, Bailey's in South Kensington. I didn't check in: I hauled my bags into a telephone booth and called, on Johnny's instructions, friends of his in London, Jerry and Nan Hochschild—he a consultant anaesthetist, she an ex-actress—who lived in Portland Place.

'Where are you?' said Nan; and when I told her I was at Bailey's she told me to stay in the foyer until she arrived to fetch me. So my first home in London was a delightful maisonette in Portland Place, my first friends the warm and welcoming Hochschilds, and my new life begun in the first post-war spring.

CHAPTER 5

FOR THE undamaged survivors the 1940s were a magical period. Danger, dread and uncertainty all behind us, the future seemed only sparkling and full of promise. The feeling of being alive was positive. We complained about rationing and the difficulty of foreign travel, then restricted, but coming out of Australia and out of the war these appeared as yet another two small adventures. It seemed to me a time of plenty, a time of wonder and excitement. If London and Londoners were tired, I was not; and I shudder to think of my Australian energy, brashness, enthusiasm, delight in the smallest fresh encounter—for they were all fresh and untainted by past experience and expectations—ploughing my way through English sensibilities. I made friends easily and quickly and discarded two of my suitors equally quickly, and brutally. I was not, in this respect, nice, kind, or even honest.

On Nan's instructions, I opened an account at Fortnum and Mason and each week they delivered my rations in a sturdy little cardboard box; the one egg cushioned between two carefully wrapped rashers of bacon and the minuscule portions of butter and cheese. These I turned over to Nan's cook; not that I remember a single meal at home in Portland Place other than breakfast. I was a spoilt and ungracious guest: as ungenerous in my grabbing at pleasure as in the breaking of ties.

I had telephoned both Johnny and David from the Bailey's call box whilst waiting for Nan: both of them on duty—one with his regiment in Scotland and the other at the Naval Signals Base at St Merryn in Cornwall. I made plans for a quick visit to Glasgow before returning to London to meet David, on weekend leave, the following week.

Just as London had filled me with excitement, Glasgow filled me with dread. Johnny was as enchanting as ever; his mother gracious and welcoming, with not the slightest hint of a tight or disapproving lip as she handed me the hand-written telegram of inordinate length she had taken down from the telephone operator. From George in Shanghai, leaving no doubt as to our relationship. No distant uncle, he. I did not attempt explanation: we both studiously ignored its contents.

My memory of Glasgow then—now one of the most culturally exciting cities in Europe—is of greyness, dark stone, windswept nondescript streets, even the places of recreation and amusement heavy with institutional pallor. The dance hall we went to amongst the elite of Glasgow seemed to me a mixture of a regimental drill hall and the Masonic Hall where I had, as an adolescent, solemnly learnt the waltz and the foxtrot. I did, however, have my first taste of fresh salmon—in those days it came only from Scotland. Canadian and Tasmanian salmon— to say nothing of the deep freeze—lay in the future. I cannot blame Glasgow for my treatment of Johnny and his no doubt supremely thankful mother, but it added desperation to my determination to cut loose as soon as I could decently claim my luggage. Allowing for my quick return to London to meet David for a joyous weekend, this took a total of three weeks: two more weeks in Glasgow and then I was free.

It remained to explain my changed status to my father. No longer 'engaged', I was once more his liability, and an allowance was arranged to keep me in England. It was £30 per month, which would, amazingly when one considers today's rates, have been sufficient for my basic needs, but was in fact secretly augmented by my mother and grandmother to Lucullan proportions. I don't remember how I explained it to Johnny.

My grandmother was bullied by my mother into selling shares, silver, anything in fact not actually bolted down or which had not already been transported to Glasgow: my mother recklessly squandered even more housekeeping money on her passion, the horses, and between them and bursts of generosity from my great aunt Juliet I managed to live in a rarefied world of

Paris haute couture and whatever frivolities London had to offer.

They were numerous and easily grasped. David and I started a weekly pattern, which was to continue for two years, until he left the Navy. I met him on the platform at Paddington Station as he got off the sleeper from Par: we rushed home to the variety of apartments and houses into which I moved, for breakfast and rapturous embraces before he left for the Admiralty and his regular Friday meetings. It had the same feeling as the blissful Fridays at boarding school when I took the train to Sydney to have the braces on my teeth adjusted and managed to cram in two whole cinema double bills before going back to school. Every Saturday night we went to the theatre, dined at Ciro's in Orange Street and wandered at midnight across Leicester Square to the '400'. Leicester Square was a gentle moonlit place in which to wander. All London seemed gentle, and benign. There will never be another nightclub like the '400', with its soft dreamy music, its enveloping quiet intimacy; the bandleader, Tim Clayton, once famous and one's friend because he played 'your tune' as you got up to dance; Rossi, the headwaiter, equally famous, who tried to give us our same table on each visit, our precious marked bottles of rationed liquor with our names on the label safely stored for us; the serene knowledge that we were young, and favoured, and alive. The room was always full of friends, glimpsed in the dark through a happy haze. One friend swears that she married her husband because on their first evening there he managed to bone her kipper in the gloom.

My first London visit to a theatre was the best possible

introduction to a world in which I was later to be involved—John Gielgud's production of *Lady Windermere's Fan* at the Haymarket. Apart from the production, I had not associated a theatre with such exquisite opulence or sense of occasion, accustomed as I was to their Australian counterparts. After that, we saw almost every West End production of the 1940s, but I am glad that the lovely Haymarket was the first and I am aghast that I never kept the programmes. The restaurants we went to on our Friday nights, now vanished, were the Belle Meuniere in Charlotte Street, all red plush banquettes and fringed candle shades, where we ate what we fondly imagined were black-market steaks—in reality, remembering the flavour, I now recognise them as horse meat; the Bon Viveur, our favourite, in Shepherd's Market where one gazed at a gaudy mural of an imaginary Mediterranean paradise while a string trio played romantic tunes on a tiny balcony; the Bagatelle, with Edmundo Ros playing, in Mayfair Place, grander and more formal, for evenings when we dressed up; round the corner the Milroy in Stratton Street, a nightclub larger and brighter than the '400', less intimate but thrilling to me because you walked down a plank over a bomb crater underneath a tarpaulin to reach it, and inside there was the joint owner, the then-famous band leader, Harry Roy himself, on the band stand and occasionally leaving it to whirl you round the dance floor; its sister restaurant opposite, Les Ambassadeurs, both started by John Mills, the Polish resistance fighter who lived to become a key figure in post-war London's restaurant and gambling world, and where you were greeted by Polish Siegi who eventually left to start his own restaurant, Siegi's, in Charles Street; the Savoy, where one would sometimes dance to Carroll Gibbons; and, of course, the Savoy Grill; and always for lunch the Berkeley Buttery. There were a variety of little lunchtime bars, too, which came and went and enjoyed their brief favour with Londoners. Tourists in the 1940s did not exist as they do now. The English were the happy tourists in their own capital. The Mermaiden Bar, running through from Dover to Albemarle Street, was a particular favourite. It was part of a now-vanished establishment called Manetta's. The bar at the Mayfair Hotel was also a favourite meeting place: and the Gay Nineties run by Eric Maschwitz, who wrote 'A Nightingale Sang in Berkeley Square', in Bruton Street, just around the corner from Berkeley Square.

My first years in London were spent in moving house, unencumbered by possessions. My grandmother's and Aunt Juliet's treasures, having been shipped down from Glasgow, had no roof to house them. A Sydney acquaintance, David Stewart-Dawson, had a warehouse—some relic of a family business—in the city. He gave me space, trestle tables laid out and bulging with the silver, china, glass. I took no interest in who came to divest me of these trappings of another life. Some payment may have been made, but I don't remember any. I saw no need in my life for one dozen Limoges oyster plates; twenty Royal Worcester gold and white tea cups; a Queen Anne silver tea service, and the like. I sometimes look wistfully in antiquarians' windows or through salesroom catalogues, wondering if I might catch a glimpse, or a hint of who may have been sipping tea or eating oysters from my dowry.

My priorities were far more frivolous in the 1940s.

The black market was a game everyone played. My black-market butcher was in Shepherd's Market: the shop, I see, is still there, although I expect our benefactor is long gone. Clothes rationing operated on a system of barter: everyone had their own pet supplier of once-worn haute couture models and we were then thin enough to wear them. Black-market restaurants were given an added fillip with the introduction of the five-shilling meal, enforced by Government Minister Stafford Cripps. We were meant to be sustained by austerity, which proved a spur to invention. I remember a sparse establishment in South Kensington bordering the Tube Station, improbably called the Imperial, whose owners may have wondered later what happened to the 'jeunesse dorée' who had flocked to their doors when word got around that one could stretch the five shillings to satisfying levels. My mother's food parcels from Australia were much sought after—toheroa soup from New Zealand, and passion-fruit, the acme of luxury. How lucky most of us are to still have serviceable livers when I recall the afternoon drinking clubs, chief among them the Tree Trunk in Albermarle Street, where we arrived at 3 o'clock, when licensing hours shut us out of the bars, and stayed, drinking lethal gins, until 6 o'clock. There was always a pianist (one of them was Gerald Lascelles, cousin of the present Queen), and although it seemed that nobody worked, or thought of work, I suppose we were gathering resolve to start up again in a more sane world. Most of our friends were 'on leave', still in uniform, or waiting to be demobilised, and, imperceptibly, they became members of professions permanently at leisure, should they wish it, in the afternoons—writers, painters, actors, and a fair smattering of the simply rich. I wonder what protected us from becoming alcoholics or drug addicts; perhaps it was the frivolity itself. The future no longer appeared threatening; only an anticipated adventure. Goethe's 'divine frivolity' was our antidote to any possible depression.

In June of that year, with David being established there for the foreseeable future, I visited Cornwall for the first time. I had both his dog and his car in London, and we would set off on those weekends when David was on duty, sometimes in leisurely fashion along the country roads—motorways an undreamt-of German-sounding phenomenon—staying the night halfway. Or take the night sleeper from Paddington and tip the guard to allow Simon, a golden cocker spaniel, the most neurotic dog I have ever known, into my bunk for the night. Through these beginnings, Cornwall has come to mean for me the 'home' I think of when I think, away from her, of England: just as the streets of Sydney are, in my heart, my other home. All else, even though tethered by affection, is temporary.

I realise now that, thanks to Johnny, David and some parental indulgence, I saw England from a viewpoint of some privilege. Of the social conditions of those years I only saw the bright side. Social consciousness was a term whose meaning I had never even contemplated. This did not mean that I was unaware of how the majority lived. I had in my childhood seen a great deal of this but only through their contact with my family and always cushioned by, if not love, then certainly compassion: our servants cushioned by my mother's and my grandmother's compassion, with perhaps the ever-present laughter in our house providing an antidote to what may have been the bleakness of their lives; and my doctor father's patients, from the worst slums of the city, always dependent on and sure of his care and concern. I expect I thought, if I thought at all, that such a comfort blanket existed in the lives of everyone.

Unlike the majority of young Australians who travelled to Europe, I did not belong to a group or mix with other expatriates. I never ventured as far west as Earl's Court or bought Australian newspapers. I don't believe I thought I would ever see Australia again, so enticing was life in London, and I didn't miss my family. My mother and grandmother both wrote to me two or three times a week. Life was a prolonged holiday which I did not envisage ever ending.

Through David, I made one half of the friends who for the last seventy years have anchored my life, and got to know, in varying degrees of intimacy, an astonishing number of interesting, famous, or infamous people—astonishing only in that I neither recognised this at the time, or, if I had done, did not think it important. They drifted into our lives in countless parties, cities and circumstances; their acquaintance enjoyed, their brief friendships embraced, but not, by me, cultivated.

The other half of my base of friendships sprang from a

telephone call made to a friend of a friend of my mother's in my first week in London—and later the two strands leading from her and from David mingled and interwove themselves into the only background an exile will ever know; a background begun arbitrarily at the moment of separation from roots.

This friend was a woman of great individuality, Violet Eaton, some twenty years older than myself, but for whom age meant little. I had telephoned her from the flat in Portland Place during my first week in London, having written in advance to announce my arrival. Vi, a passionate devotee of the dance floor, had, after receiving my letter, waited especially in London for my call instead of going back to her country house, anticipating a night at the '400', as she shared this passion with my mother's friend and could not imagine why any young man would be foisted on her unless he were a good dancer, and unattached. Her voice, when she realised that 'Robin' was female, registered shock, but, gallantly garnering what benefit she could from this Antipodean package, she suggested an afternoon at her bridge club (her other passion). This, she thought, must be the reason for Audrey's unwanted visitor. The shock that I did not play bridge—scarcely discernible in her voice—registered in full when we met: coffee at Gunter's having finally been proffered by Vi in desperation. I wasn't a man. I didn't play bridge. I was all of twenty-four. We got on wonderfully well over coffee. Vi discovered I was to spend the weekend with David's mother in a neighbouring village. David and I were invited to drinks and there I re-met an early childhood friend, Margaret Vyner, now married to the actor Hugh (Tam) Williams. So Maggy and Tam, Vi and their other friends, became overnight my new family—my links with childhood, my refuge at Christmas, my gateway to the other fifty per cent of English friends made through them.

David's mother, Nada, was a woman of immense charm and personality and, bearing in mind her own background of the much-publicised scandal of the Gloria Vanderbilt custody case in which she was found in bed with Little Gloria's mother, was unlikely to have disapproved of my own very minor 'scandal', although I had not hidden under a cloak of seeming respectability and had chosen to opt for divorce. I was taken to meet her first at lunch at the Berkeley, shortly after my arrival, found her delightful, amusing, and immediately friendly. She told David that she liked me very much and I was invited to their country house near Maidenhead the following weekend.

On the way down in the car, David gave me two casual warnings. At lunch would be his uncle who had been 'let out' for the weekend and David hoped his behaviour wouldn't be too strange. Usually, or at least periodically, I learnt, he was 'locked up'. The periods coincided with manifestations of various forms of mania, once or twice involving the use of a carving knife. Even in the raffish surroundings of Sydney's Kings Cross in which I had grown up I'd not encountered this—in my own family, Great Uncle Harry's undoubted oddity had seemed harmless enough. He had only been 'dropped on his head'.

That wasn't all. David's sister, Tatiana, had a 'keeper', an elderly female gnome, whose task, I was soon to learn, was not to let Tatiana out of her sight.

It was a particularly jolly lunch. David's uncle sat with a small square white handkerchief on his head imitating Queen Victoria, and subsequently rolling on the lawn. His mother retired to her room for a rest whilst David and I went for a walk and Tatiana leapt from behind bushes pushing our heads together and entreating us to kiss, before being dragged away by the custodian. We had started off great friends.

CHAPTER 6

THAT FIRST summer of 1946, the first peacetime summer, David had two weeks leave and we decided to visit the Mediterranean, for me only imagined through staring at the picture postcard wall at the Bon Viveur. We went by train, via Paris. The trains were decrepit, held together by rattling bolts and pieces of wire it seemed—best not to look out the window. There were no restaurant cars, no sleepers, very few seats not occupied by troops still being moved around Europe. We shambled, if a train can be said to shamble, through the shell-scarred towns and villages, hot and tired and happy, David sitting on his suitcase in the corridor and I on the lap of an obliging soldier. Deep red rocks against deep blue sea—the first glimpses of the sea in the Var region—are still for me the instantly summoned memory of that year.

The Hotel du Reserve at Beaulieu reopened after the war the week we arrived. We were the first guests, our room number 22 was the prettiest, and the manager, M. Potfer, welcomed us as the first sign of returning normality. Forever afterwards he called me his good-luck mascot. I am glad that I would not want to go to La Reserve now: it is ruinously expensive—different people, different atmosphere, different world. Its first impressions, though, stay with me as fresh as ever. I had never had melon for breakfast before, never had champagne in the bath, never seen a woman lie bare breasted in the sun, never known that in France, as part of a couple, you could register in a hotel with your correct name and not a falsely assumed marital one—something not done, if not illegal, in England and unheard of in Australia.

At the end of two weeks David had to report back for duty and we braved the rattling old train again. This time it let us down. Twenty-four hours after we embarked it panted slowly into the Gare Saint-Lazare, barely half an hour before our boat train was due to leave the Gare du Nord. The taxi which sped us across Paris arrived as the barriers clanged shut. The train stood tantalisingly on the platform. We pleaded in vain to be allowed to run for it. Finally, David shouted, '*Mais je suis l'officier du Navy Brittanique et je sera A.O.L.*' The guard lifted the barrier just enough for him to squeeze through saying grudgingly: '*Alors—allez—mais Madame et le baggage doit rester ici.*'

Like Linda in Nancy Mitford's novel *The Pursuit of Love*, hot, hungry, tired and dirty, I sat on our pile of suitcases and wept. I was rescued, not by a dashing French duke, but by a kindly porter who deposited me with a mercifully honest taxi driver. Luckily I had my own passport and just enough money for the taxi ride. He took me to a passably comfortable and totally respectable hotel in the Rue Boissy-d'Anglas. I booked a room, and rang the only telephone number I had in Paris, that of the parents of Nicki d'Ivangin, a young Russian dancer who had been dear to me and my family all through the war in Australia and who had recently died.

Nicki's brother answered the phone, delighted that I was in Paris, thrilled to meet me at last—and fortuitously able to collect me in half an hour. I had time for a hurried wash and, starving, desperate for some coffee, I waited on the pavement outside the hotel.

Nicki's brother, when he arrived, was resplendent in the outfit of a Thomas Cook tour operator. He was in the company of some thirty-odd American tourists, and he escorted me proudly to the front of the bus, which was en route to Versailles for the day. I was too young and too tired to protest, and so, in a state of consciousness heightened by hunger and exhaustion, I learnt all about Marie Antoinette.

In the four days I remained in Paris I learnt, too, much about the Paris of the Russian émigrés. We went, *en famille*, to visit Nicki's grave, in the Russian cemetery at Saint-Genevieve-des-Bois, on the very day a close colleague of Rasputin's assassin,

Prince Yusupov, was being buried. I met many of the mourners, some of them relations of David's, and through the d'Ivangins I met many more Russians: princesses who were head vendeuses at the haute couture establishments; noblemen who were secretaries at the grand men's clubs; waiters and taxi drivers who were not all princes but who, for the most part, behaved like them. And I was reunited with Wolfgang, whom I'd last seen in Australia, Nicki's dearest friend.

I owe a large slice of my life to Wolfgang Cardamatis, a half-Greek, half-German painter, who, since his teens, was brought up, under protest, in Australia. He dropped the 'Wolfgang' some years later, after he shed his German passport, and adopted one of his seven other names—in reality Johannes, but now simply 'Janni' and therefore more Greek. I owe him years filled not only with gaiety and hilarity but also with depth and knowledge. I learnt from him almost all I know and from which I derive pleasure: of great paintings; of minor art; of the conscious use of observation; of the stones of Venice as felt and seen by an inhabitant of that magic city. He taught me how to see with joy. I owe him, too, my one brief Venetian love affair, without which I believe one must feel cheated; for he lent me for the occasion—indeed orchestrated its happening—the beautiful young man with whom he was then living. Wolf was not possessive in his affections. He wanted everyone he loved to love each other.

I owe my best times in Paris as well as the later ones in Venice to Wolf. After Nicki's death, he lived there in a series of attics, by his wits and his charm and unashamedly off his friends for years. When David and I arrived he was always waiting at our hotel for a drink, a meal, a bath, and to entertain us and to show us a Paris we would not otherwise have known. If we drank too much a great deal of the time as I fear we did, we were drunk, too, with youth and excitement. I owe to Wolf my one encounter with Picasso, just as I owe to my youth the fact that I failed to benefit from it. I owe my unthinking enjoyment to the fact that I was a woman.

One summer, Wolf was living in Antibes, and his newest friend, Mario Ruspoli, a young Italian prince, was living next door. We three became firm summer friends, whilst up in the hills Picasso was organising his first show of pottery and the beginnings of his gallery. We helped him hang his canvases and display his plates and it never occurred to me to ask for so much as an autograph. Or, far better, a plate. But I did find time for a brief and delightful romance with Mario.

Wolf lived for a while in a garret in Paris with a ginger kitten called Cleopatra, who ate only fillet of sole, or the occasional breast of chicken. Cleo's upkeep eventually became too taxing, so Wolf rose one dawn and deposited Cleo warm and secure in her lidded basket on Colette's doorstep—secure in the knowledge that she would be taken in. Many, many years later I had occasion to visit Maurice Goudeket, Colette's widower, and I longed to ask him if he remembered the arrival of Cleo, but our conversation was for the purpose of establishing some copyright in Colette's work: Cleo seemed too frivolous an intrusion.

Wolf and Nicki and I had been a firm threesome in Australia:

Wolf and I now became like brother and sister in Paris and London. Paris in the 1940s was somewhere David and I went whenever he had leave and often I stayed behind with Wolf for a few days. Paris in the 1940s was perhaps more than anywhere in the world the embodiment of the feel, smell and sound of that vibrant decade. I know, now, from other people's histories what a demoralised and tired decade it was, but for me it was vibrant.

I didn't, of course, realise that in spending my nights at the then-famous nightclubs—at Vieux Colombier, at Madame Arthur's, at Scherezade, at Jimmy's Bar and in listening to, drinking with, laughing with, dancing to: Juliette Gréco, Jacques Becker, Claude Luter, Charlie Parker, Stéphane Grappelli, all then famous in the musical world—I was at the centre of something special, short-lived but resounding. It was special to me, but I saw no significance, outside the moment. I do remember how wonderful Juliette Gréco was in her ordinary black dress and with her extraordinary long nose, before Darryl Zanuck, haute couture and fashion diluted her originality. I do remember the gaiety and urgency of Claude Luter's music, and the sad, doggy little face (because I have it with me in a photograph) of Eartha Kitt, coming to the transvestite boîte, Madame Arthur's, after her own performance as one of a troupe. At Madame Arthur's, the audience frequently ran out by the back entrance as the police stormed in by the front. I remember the violins playing at one's table at Scherezade, and the fact that caviar was for the general. I remember going to Jimmy's Bar with Jimmy Donohue, notorious U.S. society figure; La Grenouille in Montmartre and the usually drunken proprietor, Roger; and Patachou who cut off all the men's ties at her bar across the way. I remember famous singer Suzy Solidor asking me to tea, and I neglecting to go.

Days shopping at the *marchés aux puces* I recollect from the random purchases made before I had any dwelling of my own; they are now much treasured and providential possessions. The canary still sings in its gilded cage; the painted tin watering can, though battered, has a distinguished air to it; the glass bottle in the shape of a gun is, I expect, a collector's item, for there are people who collect bottles. Before the Rue Jacob was as fashionable or as expensive as it is now, I bought frivolously and copiously: frivolous because I had no permanent home and the nature of my purchases—an inlaid chess table, massive brass firedogs, an Empire causeuse, a green woollen carpet with bright upstanding wired white and yellow daisies—were hardly suitable for a nomad who didn't play chess. I sold, eventually, the chess table for a regretted pittance. The carpet, before I had realised its rare and singular charm, was plucked bare of its woollen daisies by careless youths and eaten bald of its grass by energetic moths. Only the dogs and the causeuse have survived in constant use.

With my monthly allowance, and egged on by Wolf, I shopped at Jean Dessès' for dresses, at Jeanette Colombier and d'Albouy for hats, at Guerlain for scent. One night at a restaurant a waiter brought a note to my table: 'Thank you for wearing my dress so beautifully,' it said, and was signed 'Jean Dessès'. I smiled at M. Dessès, then threw away the note—and shortly thereafter gave away the dress.

All the couture houses were eager for custom and the excitement was heightened by the fact that they had been in hibernation throughout the war. I chose the house of Jean Dessès as my particular pet because early on I had met the head vendeuse, a charming and elegant lady called Jacqueline Harrari, and we were fortuitously the same size. I dressed in the height of fashion on every penny of my allowance from Australia, either through clothes brought over to England on Jacqui's back and thereby free of both customs and rationing or through trips to Paris, long hours of fittings and almost as long snippings on my part of all the grand labels, which—if left intact and of course if I had retained any of the clothes—would now garner me a small fortune. These beautiful creations were thereby shorn of their identity—I didn't even keep the labels. My loyalty to Jean Dessès suffered a brief lapse when Christian Dior burst upon the fashion world with his 'New Look'. I bought two of his first creations, discarded the labels before braving customs, as our foreign currency allowance was then still restricted to £25 per annum.

On those frequent trips to Paris, usually with David, and sometimes when left behind with Wolfgang, and therefore into trouble, I also shopped madly for hats. Hats were mad, in those days, but they were exquisite things and somewhere in the back of a cupboard I have one solitary example which has survived—a little brown felt beret with the label 'Albouy', miraculously still attached. There was a wonderful confection by Jeanette Colombier—black tulle and jet and soaring plumes and eye veils which also survived in a cupboard for some years, until discovered by Wolfgang and made into quite another creation.

A Slovakian refugee sculptor who had made his name in Australia, Arthur Fleischmann, tracked me down a year or so after I had arrived in London, asking for introductions. Prince Philip (then plain Lieutenant Mountbatten, just prior to his marriage) was dug up by me, and David's Uncle Dickie (Lord Mountbatten) and Fleischmann went to work. In no time, he was under Royal patronage and busy, rich and famous. He telephoned to say he wished to show his appreciation to me for having 'launched' him and was about to offer me a token of this appreciation. I thought of furs, diamonds—several Jean Dessès dresses, perhaps. The good man wished, however, to sculpt me. It was an excessively hot summer. Afternoon after afternoon, David drove me to his baking studio where I posed under the glaring summer light. When finished, it looked pretty, far too pretty for me, and in any event I had nowhere in my life to put it. Its pouting terracotta face remained in shadows, under stairs and in cupboards for some years. One day Wolfgang dug her out of the cupboard and by night she was transformed into a person. The terracotta face was covered in Max Factor pancake make-up, rouge, false eyelashes and my very expensive (and fashionable) chignon. My grandmother's jewellery and Aunt Juliet's lorgnettes hung around her neck; crowning it all was the black jet and net Jeanette Colombier. Looking back, she was a beauty, but she lived on, as a joke, unappreciated, on my bookcase for months: a figure of fun and a conversation piece. When tired of this, she went back, scrubbed, into a cupboard. The hat was, I expect, discarded in a dustbin and the chignon given over to the moths...

She had a third life, some years later. My doctor husband found her, fell somewhat in love with her and put her on the top of his desk. (We never could get all the Max Factor out of the cracks: she has an interesting and unusual complexion for a terracotta lady). Now, she is in my bookcase, soberly adorned with just one necklace, and people ask who she is: no reflection on Arthur Fleischmann, only on me. I looked like her once.

It was a time when David, Wolf and I took three of the iron chairs from the grass verge then bordering the Champs-Élysées, and sat in the middle of the avenue, forcing the cars to drive around us. It was a time when nobody thought of arresting us. It was still the time when cars were hoisted on to the cross-channel ferry by cranes.

There is much more opulence now, in our materialistic Western world: no recent memories of hardship, death and danger, less excuse for abundance taken recklessly.

I savoured the experiences—I liked my new acquaintances, I was enchanted with my possessions, it was all enormous fun— but I did not appreciate the singularity of my luck, singular because that particular brief era of excellence will not come again in my lifetime, and probably not that of my children.

At the end of my first year in London, George Silk followed me from Shanghai. I was still living in a tiny one room flat in Kensington Close found for me by Nan. I could not believe that I had ever seriously—or even fleetingly—contemplated marriage to George, nice and attractive as he was, but I felt very responsible for his presence. He, on the other hand, having come all this way, was determined to resolve the matter one way or the other. It was the weeks before Christmas. George became impatient with my prevaricating, my obvious lying on the nights when David was in London and I didn't want to see him, and my chronic inability to say a definite 'no'.

He hit upon the idea of flushing me out of my flat and into his life in a final spectacular gesture. Every day, in the week before Christmas, a huge Christmas tree was delivered. One just fitted into the flat, although it meant pine needles down the neck when squeezing into the bathroom. The other six or seven trees were lined up by the porters in the narrow hall. George gave up as Boxing Day dawned, and I am sure he has sometimes since reflected on his lucky escape.

CHAPTER 7

IN THE autumn of 1947 I was temporarily homeless, and invited to stay with a friend in her pretty little house in Elizabeth Street. That it was strictly her house became increasingly unclear during the delightfully *mouvementé* weeks of that autumn. We were still festooned with the tattered but deliciously gaudy remnants of war-time standards of behaviour: standards which were partly born out of a desire to please the poor boys on leave as well as a recognition that never before or again would we enjoy ourselves quite so much. Henrietta, also from Australia, had married the last of her wartime lovers but, now back in England, with her husband stationed in Germany, had not had much time to adjust to a more stable emotional climate. Also, a serving officer's pay did not compare with her peacetime suitor's fortune. Sporting a huge engagement ring where her wedding ring should have been, and with her husband hidden in Germany, she moved into the Elizabeth Street house, all expenses paid by her 'fiancé', and managed to steal a weekend free from time to time in order to visit her husband. However, a third contender appeared—a young Italian nobleman with whom Henrietta announced herself enamoured on return from a trip to Capri. The Italian, Pino, very soon followed her to London. The appointed weekend presented little problem to one of Henrietta's inventiveness: she would have one of her 'headaches' (I suspect we had both read far too many bad novels). Her benefactor, Hugo was told she must rest in a darkened room all weekend and that he must entertain himself.

Pino, when he arrived, was all Henrietta had promised— charming, good looking, and incredibly soigné with that ironed silk neatness of the Italian upper classes. As we very rarely left the pink flounced satin bower of Henrietta's bedroom anyway, we three lay chatting on the vast bed, sipping champagne prior to their evening à deux at Ciro's and the '400'. The doorbell rang. No one being expected and apprehension stirring, I was despatched downstairs to see who it was.

On the doorstep was a fresh-faced youth, pink and polite, with shining shoes and a shining smile and a small suitcase.

'I'm Gary,' he explained, 'I've come for the weekend to stay with Mrs X. Arranged by my mother. From Norfolk.'

I raced upstairs.

'Oh, my God! I forgot. His mother is a friend of mine. I said I would show him round London. Bring him up.'

Gary's introduction to London will have, I hope, stood him in good stead over the past seventy years. His first taste was drinking champagne on a bed, and a discussion as to how we would all adjust to the changed circumstances. Gary would have my bedroom at the top of the house: I would stay the weekend with a friend nearby: we would all four spend the evening at Ciro's.

The evening went well. We arranged to meet at lunchtime the next day and lunch together. I awoke to a telephone call from an actress friend, Elspeth March, who had tracked me down and who was currently appearing on stage in *Medea* with Eileen Herlie and Ralph Michael. Ralph Michael was about to have a screen test in which he had to play an Australian: he had never met one. Would I spare him an hour in which to chat? I thought I could do better. 'Tell him to come to lunch today with the girl I am living with and he can meet two of us.' Time and address given, I dressed and went round to Elizabeth Street.

In 1947, along with many other restrictions and their attendant black-market loopholes, it was virtually impossible to find anyone to do private house repairs without a permit, unless in their spare time. Henrietta had found a small firm of decorators, father and son, who were to spend every weekend painting the house. They had started that morning in the tiny hall which was totally filled by their platform ladder and pots of paint. When I arrived, Mr Perkins, père, opened the door but father and son were in some state of spluttering agitation, eyes rolling upwards. I raced upstairs to find Henrietta, prostrate on her bed and nursing her hand.

'I think he's broken my thumb,' she said.

'Who?'

'Hugo, of course. He's just been here and he has behaved shockingly. I think he's mad. Poor Mr Perkins let him in—not his fault—he's made the most frightful scene and my thumb is swelling already. It hurts dreadfully.'

Hugo had had a telephone call that morning from a kind friend who had also been at Ciro's the night before. He was therefore curious about Henrietta's headache and had come to Elizabeth Street to investigate, demanding entry from Mr Perkins and creating sufficient noise to alert Henrietta just in time to push Pino out of bed naked and protesting into a clothes cupboard, which was full, as it turned out, of my long evening dresses and high-heeled sandals—spiky ones, in 1947.

Back on the bed, black eye patch in place, Henrietta rounded on Hugo for his suspicions, his bad manners and his disruption of her peace. Frustrated and furious, he clutched at the only reliable (to date) straw in his slippery, shifting world of relations with Henrietta.

'I don't believe you,' he shouted, 'but I'll believe Robin. She'll tell me the truth!' And he stormed up the stairs to my bedroom.

Gary had had a lovely night—much of the glitter and glamour of London of which he'd dreamed in Norfolk had come true—and he was still happily dreaming when Hugo burst in.

His brief moment of consciousness ended when Hugo, not interested in the answer to his question, 'Who are you?', waited only long enough for Gary to struggle to his pyjama-clad feet before knocking him down again. In falling, Gary struck his head on the window sill and lapsed back into dreamland.

On the way down Hugo paused long enough to break Henrietta's thumb—in a struggle, she told me, to snatch off her throat the pearl necklace recently given to her, in which attempt he failed. I had arrived on his heels before Mr Perkins had had time to get back on his ladder or Henrietta to assess her injuries.

However, broken thumb or not (possibly just strained?), should we not go upstairs and see how Gary had taken the sudden intrusion? We found Gary still blissfully smiling and unconscious, but soon revived, and helped him downstairs to the communal bed. The bump on his head took precedence over Henrietta's swelling thumb, but not over Henrietta's protestations of horror and apology.

'That,' she explained, 'was my trustee. Gary, whatever must you think? I am so sorry. He is quite mad. Daddy should never have made him my trustee. He bullies me dreadfully and watches over me like a little girl. Oh, dear! Whatever will your mother say! Robin, I think what we all need is a cup of tea. Would you be an angel as you are the only one who is dressed and, indeed, not injured.'

As I made the tea I could hear Henrietta continuing to explain to Gary the necessity, financially, for Daddy to have appointed a trustee for her, and the insane zeal with which the wretched man overstepped his duties. Gary was bemused, and perhaps just a little dazed. We thankfully sipped the tea. Through the indignant monologue from Henrietta I became aware of another sound—a muffled, gasping sound from the other side of the room.

'Henrietta,' I interrupted, 'I think there's some animal in the cupboard.'

'Oh, my God! Pino!'

We raced to the cupboard. He was crouched painfully on the upturned heels of my carelessly discarded sandals, naked except for a trail of satin ribbons and the odd feather and in a worse shape than Gary. Another cup was fetched, soothing noises made all round and preparations made for going out to lunch.

'Mr Perkins,' said Henrietta imperiously, as we left the house, 'You are not to let that man in again. If anyone tries to force their way in you have my permission to throw paint over them.'

We had a restful and enjoyable lunch and strolled back through the autumn sunshine. Mr Perkins was still painting diligently. 'All well?' asked Henrietta.

'Well,' said Mr Perkins, 'Someone did try to get in and most insistent he was. When I refused to open the door he stuck his head in the letter box to look in. He had a big red beard so I sprayed that full of white paint for luck.'

Ralph Michael! I never met him. I wonder if he ever met an Australian. I wonder if he remembers. Elspeth told me it took them a very long time to get the paint out of his beard for the next performance.

CHAPTER 8

WITH DAVID I got to know quite a few kings, ex-kings, and almost-kings. This family network of royalty was a useful thread running through Europe and I learnt from my encounters the advantages of being close to royalty, now a fast vanishing breed. In their houses, one tends to eat superior meals; in their company one meets amusing and talented people (who have gathered, perhaps, for the food and the company); and, from being with them, one becomes immune ever after to the influence of those trying to impress socially. On the whole, real royals don't try to impress (with the possible exception of Princess Michael of Kent, but then she isn't a real royal).

But one of them whom I met with David late in 1946 was to influence my life from the moment of our meeting. On one Cornish weekend the officers of the naval station at St Merryn held a dinner dance, and there I was introduced to His Royal Highness, Prince Chula of Thailand, and his English wife, Lisba. They had met David the previous week and had asked to meet me when next I came down. I was invited to dinner the following night before catching the midnight train back to London, a night in the winter of 1947—the famous winter of frozen trains, lost passengers, stranded farm houses and wintry legend. We set off for dinner and I was snowed in for five days in the course of which a lasting friendship was formed.

Apart from Chula and Lisba, their Cornish ménage consisted of Bira, a then-famous motor-racing driver, and Chula's first cousin once removed: removed by one generation upwards but, because of the complicated incidence of several wives in various stages of child bearing, younger by a few years. Bira was not quite so royal, being descended not from a king and queen, as was Chula, but from a 'small' wife—as, indeed, is the present King of Thailand. He was also more purely Thai, as Chula's mother had been Russian, thereby, along with Lisba, losing him the throne, his rightful heritage: a heritage he was subsequently to be offered by the government after the death of an uncle. He wisely refused unless a referendum was held; he had no wish to be a puppet king and feared unrest from within. There was Ceril, Bira's English first wife, many dogs, and many devoted courtiers and retainers, secretaries and old friends—Russian,

English and Thai. And through the first six years of constant and close friendship and involvement in the household I came to have a sympathy and affection for the Thai people I met there.

Bira was a leading member of the international motor-racing community, and I, who now loathe fast cars and noise, became an honorary member of his White Mouse racing stable. David and I went with Chula and Lisba, and Bira and his wife Ceril, to most of the Grand Prix of Europe, helping to wave the flags and log the laps, climbing into the back of parked cars at the back of the pits for snatched moments of sleep, celebrating the races at all the Gala Balls—Bern, Monte Carlo, Belfast, Jersey, Rapallo, Reims, San Remo—sometimes in Bira's private plane.

In those days, unlike today, I was not frightened of flying. Bira's twin-engined Gemini was kept in a field near the house, so a taxi to take off involved careful avoidance of startled wandering sheep. I was prone to travel sickness. On one occasion, when Bira came to London to collect both me and David's dog, Simon, I viewed the gusting winds with apprehension. Bira gave me two large pills. I slept happily in the rear seat of the plane. Simon sat happily untethered in the front seat. Later I discovered the vet had given Bira the pills to sedate Simon.

Chula was one of the few very rich men I have known who enjoyed his wealth to the full. He spent copiously, wisely and well, and took care to see that his friends enjoyed it too. There were none of the apparent stirrings of guilt at spending or apprehension of losing it with which money curses some of the rich, nor was he dubious of the motives of those less fortunate than himself in professing friendship and affection. He and Lisba travelled constantly and in enormous style and comfort, but never alone, and they derived equal pleasure from the enjoyment of their guests. These treats were short jaunts such as David and I had to a week of lavish entertainment at the Edinburgh Festival in 1947—then sparkling new and exciting in concept—or longer trips on the *Queen Mary* or *Queen Elizabeth* to America, always with a guest or two. Shorter ones to various European countries, or even longer ones to Thailand—and even once, many years later, to visit me for three days in Australia where I was on a short stay—were meticulously planned and lovingly bestowed. At Tredethy, their Cornish house, equerries and secretaries saw to it that this ugly Edwardian house was still run on royal lines.

A typed itinerary of the weekend's events lay on one's dressing table, with the manner of dress and hour of one's required presence; a short biography of other guests was provided and punctuality demanded. Many of Chula's little quirks of behaviour strike me still as eminently sensible and thought out so as to give him the maximum enjoyment. He owned several cars but did not drive himself so that his attention was never distracted from his surroundings or company. He always sat at the head of his own table with his wife by his side, saying that as he had married her and as they seldom had the chance to dine à deux it was reasonable to suppose that he would prefer her company to anyone else's.

Both he and Lisba were intensely musical, his preference being for chamber music, and, so, four times a year, leading chamber trios and quartets were brought to Tredethy and about a hundred guests were invited, not for the intimacy of their acquaintance or the necessity of proffering hospitality, but for their enthusiasm for the musical programme.

There was a vast library, and music, fun, games, and fascinating conversation were abundantly supplied. There were always unusual incidental amusements. One of these was the dressing up in what had once been the Thai crown jewels, these having been left directly to Chula by his grandmother, the widow of an absolute monarch and thus able to dispose of her possessions as she chose. 'Granny's Belt' was a particular, and rather hideous, favourite: a solid wide corselet affair made of gold links and diamonds clasped by a huge buckle of yet more enormous diamonds. The jewels were only removed from the safe for State, or similarly grand, occasions requiring that medals should be worn, and whilst they were 'out' we would spread them around us on the drawing room floor and prance about in Granny's belt and the odd tiara.

There were other privileges to be gained from intimacy with Chula. We were escorted privately around Scotland Yard's Black Museum by the Commissioner for Police. I didn't look at the grisly bits. On our many luncheons together at Claridge's when Chula came up for the night, he would persuade me, 'Have lots of caviar. I know you like it and I'm very rich so we can afford it.' I seldom needed persuasion. Chula would fondly watch as he sipped his consommé.

I don't expect I would ever have had, or wished for, such

an extensive and intimate tour of Cambridge if Chula had not arranged it one glorious summer's day, proud as he was of his own years there. I would not have had wonderful and concrete memories of the historical events of those years and of the people who shaped them if I did not now have copies of the home movies, called Tredethy News, which were religiously recorded by Shura Rahm, Chula's Swiss/Russian major-domo, friend, and secretary. These would not qualify for film festivals but they are of abiding interest. I was living through history—we all live it— we are it—but I seem to have been lucky enough to have often been close to key moments of it, and stupid enough never to have appreciated it.

I owe to Chula my most enriching and abiding friendship, my nearest to family in my heart excepting my children. One weekend at Tredethy a fellow guest was Chula's old-time friend and one-time youthful Cambridge Don, Steven Runciman. Steven performed his party piece—the reading of palms—on all the other guests but steadfastly refused mine. His gift was genuine, and later frightened him. Then, when we were younger, it was the centre of entertainment.

On the last night of our long weekend, Chula cornered Steven and forced him into a room with me. He was not to be bullied. He took my hand in a peremptory fashion, gave it a glance and dismissed it with the chilling phrase, and a chuckle: 'I can see nothing ahead of you except long years of frustration and misery.'

A few years later, when again all other house guests had had their fortunes told by Steven and I was left out, I tried bullying him once more. This time he dismissed me with: 'You have a very good mind. I wonder why it is you never use it?'

More years were to go by until he foretold in all seriousness my husband's fate in his palm and I think I understood then why he was reluctant to look into a tragedy awaiting me.

At Tredethy, perhaps the only slight sign of displeasure to crease the royal countenance occurred if a guest showed a disinclination to strip. All guests were required to participate in the nude sunbathing in the fenced-in bathing enclosure. There was nothing prurient about these gatherings, although I am sure the good locals of Bodmin viewed them with suspicion. And they speeded up easy comradeship. When one is introduced to a stranger, be they local vet or cabinet minister, totally naked, it somehow aids the consciousness to discount social defences. Acquaintances become friends more quickly—the phrase 'down to bare essentials' takes on a fresh meaning.

I first met Henry Maxwell, Chula's oldest and dearest friend, harking back to Harrow and Cambridge, when we were both naked, although Henry, playing ping-pong at the time, wore shoes and socks. He was Chula's most favoured and most frequent travelling companion and became a dear friend to me. Henry's own stories of trips with Chula added to the store of Chula's own. He once visited Queen Juliana and Prince Bernhardt in their vast palace in Holland as just such a companion. On being shown to his room on arrival, told the hour for dinner, he changed into the appropriate dress and sat and waited for someone to escort him back to a gathering point. Dinner time drew near—so near that Henry was obliged to venture forth into the maze of corridors in the hopes of finding a friendly face. Eventually he fell among familiars and found himself seated at dinner next to a distinguished looking man of around his own age. Conversation was in French. Henry kicked off by asking his neighbour his occupation. 'Moi?' replied the astonished man, *'Mais moi—je suis l'ami du famille royale.'* This label afforded Henry endless pleasure: from now on, on all his jaunts with Chula he was able to identify himself by this appropriated, and appropriate, title.

Chula was a rich fund of royal stories, many told to him by his two uncles who in turn had been kings of Thailand, both of them childless, or one boasting only a daughter. When the first, Vajiravudh, was king and the Athlones came to Bangkok on a State visit, the monarch met the yacht which had brought them in full military regalia accompanied by his younger brother, splendidly bedecked and beribboned as Admiral in Chief of the Royal Fleet. As the Athlones stepped ashore and the band struck up a ceremonial march, the king indicated his bowing brother with a flourish: 'May I have the honour to present—my Sister!'

He was proud of his English, but there is no word in the Thai language to denote the sex of a younger or older sibling—they are identified by age.

This brother, who in turn inherited the throne, was the last absolute ruler of Thailand. In 1932, democratic ambitions were beginning to stir in the country. King Prajadhipok's advisors pleaded with him to leave the country on a grand world tour, in the hope that the dissidents and protesters would lose heart and that when he returned, any threats to his person or his position would have been removed. He took this opportunity to visit, not only fellow monarchs around the world, but leaders of state in those countries who had managed to dispose of their monarch. In particular, Mussolini.

They spoke in French. Over dinner, Mussolini enquired into the domestic situation in his guest's country. King Prajadhipok demurred at first, saying that it was a complicated story—would take long in the telling—but adding that if his host was truly interested, he would attempt to explain, and would sincerely welcome Mussolini's advice from the benefit of his vast experience, he himself being quite unaccustomed to dissent in any form.

They settled over coffee. Prajadhipok outlined, at some length, the problems facing him on his return. He looked hopefully at his mentor for comment. After a long pause, in a sad voice pregnant with thought, came Mussolini's reply.

'*Majeste, c'est mauvais.*'

Since hearing this tale, I have always nurtured a rather soft spot for Mussolini, who did not waste words.

His response must have struck a fatalistic chord in his guest, for Prajadhipok promptly returned to Thailand, to be welcomed by the first of the country's many bloodless coups d'etat and became, as a result, the first democratically deposed king and the last absolute one.

The most charming king—or ex-king—I met with Chula was Umberto of Italy, of whom I don't remember much except an amusing dinner at Claridge's. Although all David's cousins, however distant, were past or present royalty, charm did not rate high on the agenda, but they must have been interesting if only because they met a lot of interesting people and therefore had lives rich in anecdote, as did Chula. But I only remember most of them because of what we were doing at the time. King Leopold of Belgium meant a summer spent on the Italian coast in 1947—or was it 1948?—water-skiing from his boat: Prince Bertil of Sweden lived just along the coast in France from where I stayed a long, hot summer on Bira's yacht, and we dropped anchor often on his foreshore, and swam ashore clamouring to be fed. I helped pull the needles of a sea urchin from the foot of Prince Alessandro Torlonia, whilst his wife, David's cousin, the Infanta Beatriz of Spain, held his hand. I would bet he only remembers the sea urchin whilst I remember him yelping. I had never heard a grown man make so much fuss. I never bothered to keep in touch or follow up the proffered invitations, although I did strike up, and keep up until her death, a desultory friendship with his amusing sister, Marina. Marina had been married to the U.S. tennis player Frank Shields, who later was to achieve more fame as the grandfather of the actress, Brooke Shields. Once we dined in Paris with the young ex-king Peter of Yugoslavia and his wife who, on that occasion, threw her powder compact at him. I cannot remember the provocation, but I can remember the restaurant, the early great days of 'San Francisco' and what we had to eat—crêpes stuffed with seafood. Great restaurants were beginning to emerge from the austerity of the war; every new taste similar to the adventure of a child's first post-war banana or orange. The crêpes had far greater impact on me than either the king or the compact.

I only met the Windsors twice. The first time was in Monte Carlo at a Gala at the Casino in the late 1940s, where David and I had joined them. They were gay then—in the old meaning of that word—her eyes electric blue and sparkling, he smiling and genial. The second time, thirty years later, was in Paris at a private party in semi-darkness in an apartment on the Rive Gauche. I was taken on after a dinner with the Alain Berheims so cannot remember the name of our host, if ever I caught it. Flamenco dancers performed for the fifteen or so of us gathered in the salon—the duchess's eyes no longer seemed blue or sparkling; they were darker and sharper—her voice snappier and querulous. He was a shambling, pathetic figure. Two sleek young men danced attendance, to one of whom Wallis Windsor exclaimed loudly as the dancing began, 'Take David home!' and, turning to the Duke, as to one of her pet pugs, 'Go home, David, go home!' He was led meekly out.

Some of my first theatre friendships, too, were made with David. With him I first met Bea Lillie in 1947. I seldom drive down Park Lane on a misty autumn evening without remembering a pea soup fog—David at the wheel of our car and Bea walking in front with one hand on the radiator and the other waving a white flag. It was Bea who took us both to a party at Noel Coward's in Gerald Row. Years later, another life later, Noel and I were to become friends, but on that night I only remember him taking me and David up to his galleried bedroom to see his paintings on the walls. I think he had just started to paint.

On that night, too, I was to meet one of the people who graced my later life with abiding friendship—the beautiful and buoyant and endearingly funny Dorothy Hammerstein, that night at Noel's with her husband, Oscar, and her daughter, Susan Blanchard. Later, Dorothy came to mean New York to me. Her exquisite houses became my New York base, where I visited her once a year as she grew older. Older but never less funny or less beautiful.

That first night was simply one of a thousand nights: of names plopping in and out of my life—now, I fear, of no significance unless brief memories throw a chink of light on to the players. A chill thought—who remembers the players?

If David was indirectly responsible for me knowing so many kings, chance and upbringing had been responsible for having met a fair smattering of heads of state. Australian prime ministers came naturally into our orbit, given the restricted circle of Sydney society. Robert Menzies was an acquaintance of my parents: I met him whilst growing up. The gaps in our prime ministerial acquaintance were the Labor PMs—anyone other than a member of the Liberal Party, Australia's conservative representatives and about as far from liberal ethos as is possible to achieve without right-wing extremism, never swam into our little pond. One heard about them actually having private lives, but these lives did not intertwine with ours. But Liberal

Prime Minister Harold Holt was a friend. He was drowned whilst surfing, his body never recovered or even partly washed up inside a sick shark: he was the subject of many subsequent rumours about espionage, CIA activities and various cloak-and-dagger explanations. Personally I always found him far too jolly a chap to ever suspect any cause other than an imprudent swim. Two other heads of state, however, convinced me long before the media began to inform the world that there need be no connection between a responsible position in world affairs and a relaxed and uninhibited private life—Bill McMahon and Jack Kennedy—both of them in my life as my bridegroom's best friend and best man at two of my weddings: one to John Spencer, achieved, and the other, to Torbert Macdonald, aborted.

Billy had been a romantic 'escort' in my teenage years. No more than bruised and swollen lips and late nights between us but enough for me to think of him forever after as simply a good dancer, and an entertaining companion—certainly not a future prime minister. When it transpired that he was also John Spencer's best friend, I added 'best man' to his tags in my memory.

For my proposed second marriage, until the priests and the family managed to extricate Torbert from his impending mortal sin, Jack was to be our witness and ally.

Jack and Torbert had been roommates at Harvard and insep-arable for years; they were in P.T. boats together in the Pacific, although Jack was shipped home before I was to meet Torbert, when he was on leave in Sydney. Our engagement lasted only long enough for Jack to be appointed best man for the wedding which was to take place as soon as I could be got out of wartime Australia to the U.S. But the Church got there first, and I did not actually meet Jack until some four years later.

In 1948 David and I were in France—he staying with his mother at her house in the hills above Cannes, I at the Hotel du Cap at Eden Roc. At the bar by the sea on my first day I ran into Torbert. He was on holiday with the entire Kennedy clan—and we joyfully joined forces. He was by now married, but insisted, naturally, as is usually the case with husbands alone on holiday, unwillingly and unhappily. I was not married to David, but, smarting under the indignity of his mother's growing disapproval and remembering the fervour and fun of my time with Torbert, it took little more than enthusiasm on Torbert's part to resume our relationship. Some nights, when David was not with his mother, I spent with him, but the rest of my time was spent with Torbert, Jack and those Kennedy sisters and brothers who were there. Individually I only remember Bobby, in his teens I think, and the baby, Teddy, and the noise they all made in the pool.

The night after we met Jack took Torbert and me to a memorable party—memorable for many reasons. The host was Argentinian Alberto Dodero, said to be the power and the money behind Juan Perón. By his side, acting as hostess, was a cute blonde young American of about nineteen.

The locale was a magnificent house by the beach at Cap d'Antibes, gardens and terraces going down to the sea, which

Dodero was said to use only for parties. He and his guests slept in an equally magnificent house up the road. Fountains played champagne. Two dance bands played different rhythms in different parts of the gardens. At each guest's place was a small token—small in size but not in value. At our table I have always believed that I watched the first meeting between Rita Hayworth and Aly Khan. Elsa Maxwell was beaming beside them and it has been reported many times that they had met earlier with her, but it seems in my memory that they met that night. Jack drank too much and fell into one of the fountains. I lost my temper with him and demanded to be taken home.

He had hired for the holiday a tiny 'Deux Cheveux'—the baby Citroen whose headlamps were so close together that we had christened it 'Stewart Granger'. (Many years later Jimmy Granger became a friend; he was very beautiful but his eyes were rather close together.) I waited, fuming, in the huge circular hall, Torbert sulking beside me, whilst Jack went to fetch the car. A footman in knee britches waited behind every one of the six marble pillars soaring to the domed ceiling.

With horn blaring and headlights full on, up the shallow marble steps came a bouncing 'Stewart Granger'. The footmen chased Jack round the pillars as he weaved between them; Torby and I jumped in and we bumped down the steps into the night, tempers and sulks forgotten.

The night never was. I read subsequently in a newspaper diary that Jack's son, aged twenty-four, pedalled up the steps of a hotel and into the foyer on his bicycle, so perhaps Jack remembered it, too, and had told the story.

We spent the next two weeks together. Jack and Torbert were sharing a suite at the Hotel du Cap. I had a cupboard in the 'combles'—normally one of the servants' rooms. So most days, for an hour or two, I sat at the desk in Jack's sitting room writing, at his dictation, to the potential voters back in the States whom he hoped would get him re-elected to Congress.

'Dear Mrs Blank,' I wrote on one of the postcards with which he supplied me each day, 'I want to thank you for all your support. I'm enjoying a much needed vacation and I do hope your husband's back trouble has cleared up/daughter's baby has arrived/mother's angina is better. Kind regards, Sincerely, John F. Kennedy.'

I often wonder if the recipients kept the cards, now have them framed, or have tried to sell them only to be told they are forgeries.

I threw away all Jack's subsequent letters to me—a few casual enough notes to London announcing his arrival, messages from Torbert, amicable details of I do not remember what— but certainly not forged. The night he became President I could hardly believe it. The night he was assassinated it seemed to be happening to someone quite other than my youthful friend. And the myths now building up around him have that same quality of unreality.

I saw no evidence then of the sexual appetite and obsession now emerging from accounts. I don't even remember any female companion. He was Torbert's friend and we were a threesome.

The sexual encounters, if happening in those early days, were kept hidden from me.

His letters to me were real enough and could since have been put to good commercial use. If I could be born again and granted one material wish it would be to live and die in the house in which I was born, a house boasting a vast attic, stored with relics and memories from the past. In those attics would be the concrete reminders of my ancestors' lives, the mysteries surrounding my parents' emotions, my own changing person, and, above all, the letters. I need not have destroyed Jack's—nor T.S. Eliot's, infinitely more interesting. I had crossed paths with Eliot briefly during my stint as 'London representative' of Swedish impresario, Lars Schmidt. This was a sinecure, rather than an arduous job, dreamt up by Lars as a means of contact and it was regarding the performance of Eliot's play, *The Cocktail Party*, in Scandinavia that we corresponded. I wish I had his letters, Jack's letters, the couture clothes I bought on our Paris trips, the lost or given-away family treasures, the proffered and never accepted presents. One letter I have kept which gave me pleasure and a frisson of pride was by Noel Coward on reading *Aunts up the Cross*. It is so typical of him that I find that sufficient excuse to quote it here: I feel, too, that the 'aunts' may have been tickled had they known that Noel Coward 'loved' them. 'My dear Robin, How sweet of you to remember to send me "The Aunts". I dearly love them and enjoyed every word...'

My worst recollected carelessness was the occasion on which, in 1947, I was taken to tea in his cottage in Cookham with the painter, Stanley Spencer, who on that and on a subsequent visit offered me any of the paintings stacked on the floor, in the sink and in the bath. We sat on packing cases while he boiled a kettle, an uncapped milk bottle at our feet. He was a strange little man, and I politely looked at the paintings, and just as politely declined. If I had taken some of the paintings, I may have been able to afford the house in which to store everything discarded.

Perhaps the worst missed—or thrown away—opportunity was my failure to celebrate the anniversary of the victory over Japan with Winston Churchill on the roof of the Admiralty. David's uncle, Louis Mountbatten, had invited David and me to join the party of VIPs gathering there. We dined first at Ciro's, and set off much too late on foot towards Whitehall, struggling against the crowd through Leicester Square and into Trafalgar Square. My subsequent horror of crowds had not manifested itself and so we joined the jostling throng, the mounted police, fainting revellers swaying under the fireworks with great good humour. Halfway there, we decided it was just too much trouble, turned back, and collapsed thankfully into the doorway of the '400'. I never met Churchill.

CHAPTER 9

IN THE summer of 1947 before the episode with Pino, Henrietta had managed to convince Hugo that she needed a healthy holiday with a girlfriend. The girlfriend chosen was, sadly, even then somewhat eccentric and has, in fact, since been committed to a mental home. However, in 1947 Pammie was able to serve Henrietta's purpose by supposedly joining her on a 'walking tour'. Weighed down with Hugo's banknotes but nothing more athletic than a few flimsy nightgowns, Henrietta and Pammie embarked on the cross-channel ferry, blowing kisses to Hugo, and were met at Calais by Henrietta's husband, with car, on leave from Germany. Pammie was sent back on the next boat. David and I contrived a holiday on the Cote d'Azur every summer, in addition to our Paris weekends, and our racing trips with Bira and Chula, so we drove down and we all four met up at our old stamping ground, La Reserve. We had all been friends in Sydney during the war. (David had told me he thought he'd been to bed with Henrietta before we had met. He was not sure having, it seemed, had quite a bit to drink, but he did remember a Chinese takeaway dinner in her apartment, and Henrietta disappearing to reappear in a black lace nightgown. The black nightgown had made such an impression that he was unable to concentrate on the remainder of the evening with similar clarity.)

Tam and Maggy Williams had rented a house down the coast; friends, Eliza and Tommy Clyde were at another one; and we all set about the business of procuring enough French francs for our holiday, it being the years of the £25 travel allowance. Only Henrietta had smuggled enough in. The rest of us were condemned to the nightly prowl at the Carlton Bar where we could meet Cedric Keogh, the leader of the pack of English law-breaking currency traders. He had direct access to one Max Intrator, who was to figure largely in the press headlines later that year. I had wangled an introduction to a Frenchman, Roger Peronnier, who came often to London, so Maggy and Tam and I acquired our francs from him. We were too late to save Eliza. She was the only one of us to actually write out a cheque direct to 'Max Intrator'—handed to Cedric under the table and later published on the front page of the *Daily Mail* when Max Intrator was caught.

'Duke's Daughter in Currency Scandal' blazed the head-lines, and Eliza was reported as having changed £3000. In 1947 £3000 was a fortune. Eliza had actually changed £300, and was fined accordingly. She successfully sued the *Mail*; damages were awarded to her. She claimed only £300 and came out square: the *Daily Mail,* no doubt, could not believe its luck.

Living through the war had accustomed us all to living on the brink—of danger, of luxury, of penury. My new friends fitted perfectly into the framework of my upbringing. Few of us earned a regular wage; none of us had saved a penny; all of us dined nightly at the Ivy, the Caprice, the Savoy Grill, and drank cham-pagne for breakfast. We took off across the channel to sunshine and more champagne and the Parisian shops with not much thought of the future bills to settle. Roger Peronnier helped to push these horrid thoughts further into the background as he seldom came to England more than twice a year. Settling up was 'mañana'.

However, one day he arrived, unannounced, and it fell to me to telephone Tam with the request for a rendezvous. Tam had had a particularly bad day at the races and so the required £400 was a bitter pill to digest after an almost forgotten summer idyll. The francs with which he had furnished us had been well spent. The Monte Carlo casino was still the haunt of international gamblers like the famed Dolly Sisters, but they were equally welcoming to 'les jeunes Anglais' as long as bills were paid. On the night that David, Tam and Tommy had all gone 'banquo' at the tables, we were cleaned out. Offers to wash up were ignored, so all our passports were impounded, rescued the next day by Roger's francs. Somehow Tam managed to scrape the sterling equivalent together: we all met for a forced welcoming drink for Roger in the Savoy Bar.

Roger pocketed Tam's envelope, bade us all a courteous farewell and went up to his room and shot himself.

We were unable to find out if the £400 was still, neatly folded, in his pocket and could only, miserably, read the news headlines about his body. He had done us proud and we felt guilty that we had not given him a jollier send off...

* * *

I had my allowance from home. David had his Naval pay and the allowance of £5 per week given to him, and also to his cousin, the then Prince Philip of Greece, by their uncle, Lord Mountbatten. We decided that between us we could afford to rent a furnished flat of our own. Through friends we found a charming two bedroomed flat in the Kings Road for £8 per week, of which we paid half each.

As David was able to be in London only at weekends I had ample opportunity to make many new friends, and of these, one was to become central to my life. This was the photographer, Baron, then the first of the eminent photographers to be socially 'acceptable', barring Cecil Beaton. He owed this partly to his unique and lovable personality, partly to his connections, and not a great deal to his talent. In youth, he and the then young

Dickie Mountbatten had both been in love with a fascinating French woman, Yola Letellier, and they had met at her feet in Paris. They had remained friends: in time, Uncle Dickie had introduced Baron to his nephew, Philip, and in turn Philip introduced him to David and me.

Baron (his full name was Baron Nahum, but he was always known as Baron) became one of my dearest friends: we spoke every day on the telephone until his death. Through him I met and mixed with many of the London characters of the 1940s, a third world to add to the royals and the theatre people—nights at the Pheasantry with Augustus John, who literally chased me 'round the table of the proprietor's back room; at his studio with Feliks Topolski, where I experienced my first and last lesbian approach. Such was my Australian inexperience in those years that I didn't fully realise its meaning. It was not at all unusual in 1947 for innocence to go hand in hand with a certain amount of experience. Vi Eaton, who, for years, lived a peaceful and workable 'ménage à trois' with husband and lover, was nonetheless totally ignorant of some facets, rather than the basic facts, of worldly life. Two homosexual men friends were coming to stay: bedrooms to be allocated, the supply of single beds a problem.

'Let them share a double bed,' said her husband, 'That's what they would prefer.' Vi was astounded: 'I always thought they did it standing up!'

Baron told me later that I had sat gingerly on the edge of a sofa acting like a Lady Mayoress of Kensington whilst a drunken Barbara Skelton attempted to pull down my pants. She sat on the floor at the feet of a tall, dark glamorous girl, another Barbara, whose second name I don't remember but who was an habitué of our 'circle' because she was the girlfriend of a genial American living in London, Fred Tupper, then the PR representative of Pan American Airlines. The two Barbaras were enjoying themselves in what appeared to me a most curious fashion, indulgently watched over by Felix and Baron, before Barbara Skelton turned her attentions to me. Baron took pity on my prim lips, murmured protestations and firmly crossed legs and took me home. I don't remember seeing Barbara again and now having read her books of reminiscences regret not having known her better, although perhaps not in the guise first offered to me. She went on to marry writer Cyril Connolly (twice) and publisher George Weidenfeld, and I never got into close sexual proximity with a woman again.

Baron was, in due course, to give me away at my wedding and become godfather to my daughter but he was indeed reputed to be at the centre of a very 'fast' world indeed. One heard lurid tales of orgies. With me he was a loving and gentle friend. We met when David had gone skiing for two weeks and asked Baron to look after me. Introductions to Baron's friends opened up avenues of enjoyment; painters, writers, photographers—skimming the surface, I now realise, of a murkier world underneath, of which I remained innocent.

His best friend, the painter Vasco Lazzolo, discovered a magic pill which was supposed to make us all madly sexy. You put it underneath your pillow and at the crucial moment of intercourse you were supposed to pop it and inhale. David and I tried it once, it didn't appear to do more than slow up proceedings. One was always losing them under the pillow. I think they were yellow and I expect they were the first primitive precursors of amyl nitrate: known, I believe, as 'poppers'.

After the first year and the first flush of enthusiasm shown to me by David's mother, an icy curtain had descended over her initial warmth. I never discovered the exact reason but have since been told that I was considered 'fast' and a bad influence on David, and indeed was the subject of a flurry of worried correspondence between his two aunts, Lady Zia Wernher and Queen Louise of Sweden.

I think the true reason for the cooling was that I had no fortune, or prospect of one, with which to augment his frugal Naval pay. The bad influence was farcical. Apart from Torbert, the fleeting Americans and the horrid experience of John Spencer, I certainly had known little else of the great wicked world. I was an innocent abroad and it was David who introduced me to a world I had not dreamed existed: louche photographers, popping pills, and new experiences.

I also tried, in a fashion necessarily desultory because of the frequent attraction of taking off on trips, to settle down. My parents never suggested, nor even hinted, that I should work, but the allowance needed to be augmented if the trips were to continue and the couture houses not given up. I looked around for work which did not entail regular hours, or even days, and which would allow me to come and go as I pleased. Needless to say, this led to a startling turnover in jobs.

A newspaper column seemed the ideal. I had written a precocious one for a time in Sydney, with copious and amateurish illustrations; this was little more than a weekly diary of my doings. I had no difficulty in persuading the same editor, Eric Baume of *Truth* newspaper, that I could provide a fascinating résumé of the week's events in London. Delivery was on Wednesdays. Baron took the portraits which headed my column. I rose at 6 a.m. on Wednesday mornings and dashed off my few hundred words, culled mostly from my engagement book (a life crammed into tiny pages—Christian names only—sometimes luncheon or dinner on several consecutive days with a Mark, an Otto, or a Douglas. Who were they, one wonders, and where are they now? And how do they remember the forties? Perhaps, like me, they have difficulty remembering them at all.)

These working stints could never be considered taxing. The London of the '400' and Ciro's, Ascot and Henley co-existed alongside the London of the Pheasantry, the marvellous institution in the Kings Road, and the Gargoyle in Soho, a more bohemian, intellectual watering hole—and into this world I was introduced by Baron, and new friends. One of these—with whom I had, together with many of the available and unavailable women in London, a romance, deepening through the years into a friendship—was Mark Culme-Seymour. Mark was spectacularly good looking, hopelessly charming, and tended to marry the oddest people: elderly princesses whom he erroneously thought were rich, or waif-like creatures, even more adrift than himself.

The marriages did not last long. In between them, Mark and I spent many nights in the Gargoyle, some of those nights drinking with Guy Burgess and occasionally Donald Maclean, of whom I recall little except their drunken arguments.

The column continued for about a year. I tired of it before they did, probably because more intriguing opportunities opened up which did not necessitate the early Wednesday mornings.

More rewarding was a monthly travel piece I wrote for Sydney Ure Smith's prestigious little magazine *Art in Australia*. This allowed me to push guilt to the back of my mind as I whirled off to Göteborg, Oslo, Belfast...Reading, fifty years later, some of these diaries and travel articles, I am struck by history repeating itself, swept back by memory into immediate post-war England, reminded of our material obsessions, deprivations and of our differing freedoms. Different ones, now: the crises are comfortingly the same—only the leading players have changed names.

The social jottings, now embarrassing to read, are nevertheless a pleasant memory jolt: the travel articles of more interest, not for my reactions but because they are history; I remember little of it. I went to Dublin with George Silk, to Paris with David, to Göteborg with Lars Schmidt: only reading through these old articles do I realise what we were experiencing and how little of it is left.

Not surprisingly, David, too, had his rare lapses from fidelity, but his, always confessed, were usually one-night affairs propelled by alcohol and devoid of romance. Emotionally, he never wavered in his loyalty to me. This did not mean I was not furiously jealous. As two of them were with Hollywood actresses after some celebrity party to which I had not been invited, I never met them, but the third was an eighteen-year-old bouncy blonde, introduced into our circle by Baron and generally considered anybody's. At the party subsequent to David's confession, I glared at her with hatred and contempt—both melting into liking on hearing her talking to Baron, Vasco and some friends. Painter Vasco had criticised Baron's photographic skills. Sunny leapt to his defence.

'How can you say that! He's a famous photographer!'

'Well,' said Vasco, 'that's not saying much. I'm a famous painter but I'm not a very good painter.'

Sunny thought for a moment. 'Oh, I see what you mean. I'm really not a very good fuck.'

CHAPTER 10

NOT CONNECTED with my own journalistic attempts, but through two friendships, with John Hannay and Jeannie Nichol, I had entered another world of intimacies—the inhabitants of London's Fleet Street. Johnny was a regular feature of the Williams household. During my first year he had become my friendly weekday escort when David was on duty in Cornwall, and I incited Tam's irritation when I refused his tentative proposal of marriage. 'Why can't you marry him? I'm sick to death of him being in love with Margaret.'

Tam was responsible for my second marriage proposal of about this time. Another constant member of our group, a customary fellow guest at the Williams' Christmas gatherings, was the actor Guy Middleton. Guy was attractive, amusing and not known for his hospitality. He was inclined to go to the loo as his turn came for a round of drinks. One day Guy rang and asked me to dine at l'Ecu de France in Jermyn Street, one of the better restaurants of the 1940s. A chauffeur-driven limousine was sent to fetch me; a rug was tenderly laid across my knees. Something afoot, I thought. Not far into our meal Guy made his proposal. He thought it high time he got married and, looking around for available candidates, had alighted on me. No romance involved this time. After I dismissed this idea as absurd, Guy lapsed into snappish gloom and I was sent home in a taxi. The following morning Tam telephoned. 'Did you accept him?' he wanted to know. It seems Guy had asked his advice and Tam, thinking of our Christmas numbers and the wish to keep them in the family, had suggested me, which Guy had thought not such a bad idea.

Johnny was working for the Savoy group of hotels, and subsequently was made a director when, calling on his war-time experience in the Special Forces and his wartime buddies, he was responsible for breaking the oil miners' strike which threatened all London and would have broken the back of the Savoy. It was an opportunity to get out—if not the tin hats—then a few old army revolvers and some khaki overalls, borrow some army trucks, and drive them through the night from the north of England with enough oil to keep the hotel going. We, his camp followers, watched from the hotel's upper windows and cheered as the lorries braved the pickets and crashed through.

Johnny, as director, provided a second home for me at the Savoy; a wardrobe (still in situ) from the Berkeley Hotel when I was furnishing my first apartment; a daily bath at the Savoy when the pipes froze in the winter of 1947; and my introduction to Jeannie Nichol. Jeannie later became well known through her own books about the Savoy and her husband Derek Tangye's books about their life at Dorminack at Land's End in Cornwall. In 1946 Jeannie was still press officer at the Savoy, Derek was still a working journalist, and she became my closest friend. We were of a similar age and temperament. Her office was the centre of gaiety as well as information, and the famous Fleet Street columnists made it their base. Christiansen of the *Express*, Noel Barber, Noel Monk of the *Mail* (a fellow Australian), Don Iddon from New York and Bertie Gunn (father of the poet Thom Gunn) are some of the names I remember from our daily gatherings in the Savoy Bar. All the celebrities of the 1940s who made the Savoy their base made Jeannie's office the heart of that base.

Jeannie and I started a luncheon club—in competition with the Thursday Club. The Thursday Club was the brainchild of Baron: amongst its members were his twin Jack Nahum, the painter Vasco Lazzolo, Prince Philip, David, Pip Youngman Carter, then editor of the *Tatler*, Philip's private secretary Michael Parker, actor James Robertson Justice, harmonica player Larry Adler, and any male of interest who happened to be in town. They lunched at Wheeler's in Old Compton Street. Thursday night was a lost cause if you happened to be the wife or girlfriend of any of the members.

We were determined to wreak our revenge on at least one man every Wednesday, and so our club was born. We invited a man to lunch each Wednesday. In the morning, a red carnation was delivered to the man of our choice: he was to present himself at one o'clock at the Bon Viveur in Shepherd's Market: and before he was decanted at sundown he was to write a piece in our club book. A.P. Herbert (Sir Alan Herbert, writer and MP) wrote our club rules, and we entertained many of the visiting journalists from America—including A.J. Liebling and Sam Boal—comedian Danny Kaye, and all our London friends and acquaintances. Alan's rules read:

RULES (if any)
1. There shall be two original members, namely: Robin Spencer, Jean Nicol.
2. The original members shall, in no circumstances, pay any subscription—a privilege to be reserved for New Members.
3. At all Ordinary Meetings there shall be one guest only, a Man, who shall be alone, defenceless, and decanted with a Red Carnation.
4. There shall be an Annual Meeting, at which the refreshments shall be provided by the Guests.
5. The general tone of the Club shall be hostile to the use of alcohol.

In addition to writing the club rules Alan became both

intrigued and incensed by the lurid story of my divorce, and the truth behind it. Alan had been a driving force behind changes to the antiquated divorce laws and now worked at some amendments. He worked at it tirelessly and eventually with success in Parliament, and it is gratifying to reflect that hordes of British women now owe their freedom from brutal husbands indirectly to my teenage trauma.

* * *

London was beginning to attract tourists again—peacetime tourists who wanted proper places to live and guidance about where to shop. So 'Contactus' was my next foray into work. Siegi Sessler—the Polish restaurateur who with his fellow Pole from the Polish Armed Forces John Mills, who had started Les Ambassadeurs—had formed his own immensely popular club restaurant, Siegi's. There was a suite of three rooms on top— empty—and a restaurant below, full nightly of people asking Siegi where they could shop, hire a car or rent a flat. I moved into the three rooms by day: we had cards printed with Contactus emblazoned on them, and I wrote some very peppy sales talk to go with it. We did very good business. The restaurant was in Charles Street: David and I and whoever else I was with, ate at the restaurant for nothing. By this time I had moved into Mount Street nearby, and it was all very pleasant. We were the first of such agencies to start up in London, and had I had the staying power or the ambition to continue it might still be going strong.

In London, occasionally, a friend from home would arrive but not until the 1950s did they appear in any numbers.

They were my fleeting links with home, tethered by shared memories. During the war, at one of my mother's Sunday night gatherings, Peter Finch, the actor, had managed to find the bathroom, but, in his haste, not the bathroom light. Nor the lavatory. Relieving himself in the bath and hearing a dull and muffled thud rather than a metallic tinkle, he groped for the light. My mother had stacked the bathtub with bowls of trifle. Those of us to whom Peter recounted the accident declined pudding.

Finchy was an endless source of stories. Before he left Australia for England and fame, he became engaged to a friend of ours. The wedding was to be a fairly prominent social event: no veil but at least a bridesmaid; and society gossip columnists. Everyone turned up except Peter, who caught the train to Melbourne instead. When he later married his lovely Russian ballerina wife, Tamara, it was from my family's house as my parents were the nearest he had to a family in Australia. He had been born in England, and was more or less abandoned in Australia by both parents.

I had been in England for three years and living in a pretty house in Trevor Square when the telephone rang one evening. Eight people were coming to dinner and I had just laid the table and squeezed the eight little gilt chairs around it. It was Peter. I had not heard from him during the intervening years but his excitement overcame any need for preamble.

'I've found my mother!' he shouted down the telephone. 'I've just met her. She's terrific. I want to bring her round to see you at once. Can we come now?'

Churlish to say no: there was just time to rush round the corner to Harrods for more food and forage for two more chairs from bedrooms: squeeze all of them closer together; lay more places; and explain to other guests as the clock ticked on way beyond eating time that we were waiting for Peter.

I waited two years before I ran into him again one night. He was not with his mother and so I never met her and neither she nor the dinner were ever mentioned again.

A few other Australians contacted me—those who were, like me, to spend the better part of their lives in Europe and make their niche there in their chosen professions. Jocelyn Rickards brought one of the first of her famous (in her books as well as in their own lives) lovers, Freddie Ayer, to see me—and she went on to become a successful stage and film designer. Wolfgang brought the young Diane Cilento en route to drama school, magnificent with her original Roman nose before she snipped it and married Sean Connery. Loudon Sainthill and Harry Tatlock Miller arrived, Harry to open the Redfern Gallery, and Loudon to design some theatrical hits of the time. We each went on our separate ways—never to form a clique—thrusting out different tentacles. Only the young Michael Blakemore was to remain important, much later, in my life. He arrived on my doorstep, abandoning his comfortable Sydney background and working his way as a ship's steward, determined to become an actor, with an ambition at the back of his mind to become a film director.

I had no idea what to do with this twenty-one-year-old youth, although he now tells me I was very 'kind' to him. He went on to become a consummate actor, a wonderful writer, and a world-class theatre and film director before our lives were to mesh again.

I was busy in other areas.

CHAPTER 11

LARS SCHMIDT was a divinely attractive Swede, then in his late twenties. We met at Sandown races with a naval officer colleague of David's, Bertie Hardman. Bertie and I had known each other since Sydney: Lars had recently met him skiing. Lars and I both pretended enormous interest in horse flesh, as opposed to betting, as we broke away from the rest of the party between each race on the pretext of visiting the paddock and inspecting the horses. All through those irresponsible crazy years Lars was the only serious threat to David's position in my heart, but threat he certainly became and it did not occur to me to hide it. A certain pique had something to do with it. David had agreed in late 1947 to be best man at the wedding of his cousin, Prince Philip, to Princess Elizabeth, and from being an unknown young naval officer he was thrust into the forefront of media attentions and consequently those of socially ambitious mothers. The temptation to accept the subsequent invitations now showered on him, in which I was not always included, from various foreign ambassadresses with marriageable daughters and the like was strong. I could not really blame him when I considered how I had spent my weeknights whilst he was in the Navy. What is worse, I had been largely responsible for him leaving the Navy, urging him to give up such a regimented life, take his seat in the House of Lords, and take a job. As always, fun and freedom seemed more enticing than permanence. I wasn't so happy with the occasions when freedom meant freedom from me, and fun meant having fun without me. Lars was my riposte, although I didn't see it that way and Lars was reason enough himself.

After our first meeting in London, we arranged that I should visit him in Göteborg as soon as possible. Unfortunately, he had a wife (years later he had another better known one, Ingrid Bergman). I flew to meet him in Oslo for our first weekend together. This later bore fruit as an article for *Art in Australia*, and growing bolder we decided we could meet closer to home, combining my next article with a summer week on the Koster Islands, driving there from Copenhagen. The midnight sun never set: Lars and I arrived in Göteborg after a week lying in it, burnt black except for peeling noses—I supposedly direct from grey England as a friend of Bertie's on a brief trip to Göteborg and Lars after a supposed business trip to Copenhagen.

Through Lars, I somehow slipped into another job. He was at the beginning of his distinguished career as a theatrical impresario, and starting in those days as Sweden's brightest young literary agent, the earliest champion of his friend, Ingmar Bergman. I was to be his Girl Friday in London, on the lookout for likely plays and a contact with English authors. From this beginning came my friendship with Peter Ustinov, then a fledgling director set to direct Bergman's *Frenzy* in the theatre; and my association with T.S. Eliot through Lars' Scandinavian production of *The Cocktail Party*.

My relationship with Eliot was conducted largely on the telephone and through letters (all since thrown away). Peter and I however, shared some hilarious Swedish experiences.

We went together to Göteborg to celebrate the most important Swedish Festival, that of Midsummer's Night Eve. On this night, the first crayfish of the season are eaten. The week passed in a haze of 'Skol' and aquavit, crayfish and dill, and everyone creeping round the house in long white gowns carrying lighted candles and wearing crowns of leaves. Dressed in these, the children and women of the house burst into bedrooms at dawn crying out guttural greetings. This was superb material for Peter's comic genius to parody.

At the end of our week, a dinner was given in our honour by Lars' parents at their beautiful estate outside Göteborg, awash with more aquavit, more crayfish, and white gloved footmen behind every chair. We were toasted relentlessly by all the twenty or so guests: 'Skol'—a raised glass across the table. 'Skol' we slurred back, and another glass drained, so as not to offend.

At the end of dinner, one of the guests got to his feet and spoke at length, in Swedish; there was much nodding of heads, bowing and smiling in our direction—much more raising of glasses—much applause and twenty pairs of expectant eyes trained on us. It was obvious that this was an elaborate toast to us and that a reply was expected. Peter did not fail. He rose majestically to his feet, and at equal length replied, in faultless phonetic and incomprehensible sounds.

Our kind hosts and fellow guests were too polite to show their bewilderment. They smiled, nodded, raised more glasses and dutifully applauded.

When we left Sweden, Peter confided to me that he had actually mastered only two words of Swedish, culled from the newspaper headlines reporting his frightening flight into Göteborg when the landing gear had failed to operate: '*nervepreenderer minuten*'.

The following midsummer's eve we were in London. I had moved into the charming house in Trevor Square, and Lars insisted on us having our midsummer's Swedish celebration in Knightsbridge. The crayfish were to be shipped in that day. Peter and I were to race to the airport to collect them and the accompanying crate of aquavit. All I had to do was to provide the boiled potatoes, the dill, the glasses, and the guests. At midnight we were to raise our glasses to Lars and distant Swedish friends.

We expected our crayfish on ice; not actually in it. When

located, they glared reproachfully at us, through their ice prison, four solid blocks of it, resembling some beautiful modern sculpture—or a hundred glass paperweights compressed into one.

We had time to borrow a pile of ice picks from the Savoy, some sacking on which we deposited the four blocks; and the party took on the appearance of a roomful of mad sculptors frenziedly attacking their prey. Ice pick in one hand, a glass in the other, we hacked away far into the night, scattering headless crayfish and blood all over the floor.

When he could, Lars came to London. Sometimes David was in town—sometimes not. In the former case, introducing them seemed simpler than juggling. In those days, a small aeroplane could be hired at what cannot have been enormous cost, considering how frequently Lars did it. We hired one to go to the Grand National in 1948. It was a six seater: David was in London and it seemed churlish not to ask him along. It was a very windy day: I was very sick indeed, and the plane was not equipped with sick bags. Lars retreated to the back seat with his form guide, as far away from me as he could manage. David took his place beside me and held out his hat, and my head, as I was sick into it. Through my miserable retching I was aware of a small inversion of values and in no doubt as to which of the two of them could be relied upon in extremis.

It wasn't enough to tether me to earth. The next time, we hired a plane to go to Paris for dinner. In 1947, with rationing still in force in England, it was illegal to spend more than five shillings on a restaurant meal. Horse meat steaks at the Imperial couldn't compete with the Tour d'Argent. David was already there, visiting his mother, but I had told him I would be there for the night. On this occasion he turned up at our hotel and locked me in the ladies lavatory in an attempt to stop me leaving for the airport for our return flight.

But the pattern was set, and it was enticing, never to be rejected. So, when Eric McIlree, an Australian car manufacturer, not a close friend of my youth, but an acquaintance of many years, turned up in London in quest of the insurance due him for an aeroplane he had had shot down from under him over Vietnam (the French troubles—not the later American ones) I was ready. The insurance money was to be collected in Paris; Eric had never been to Paris. He telephoned to ask if David and I would go with him to show him around, in a plane he intended to hire for the trip. We were at a loose end (I can't remember many tied ends), and so within hours we were ready to go with Eric. We set him up with a girlfriend—a friend of mine living in Paris—on his first night, and in eight days the four of us managed to spend the best part of the crashed plane.

It must have seemed worth it to Eric, for within months he reappeared in London, on the telephone again, leaving that day in yet another hired plane for another night in Paris. This time, Lars was in London: we had an hour in which to change our plans for the evening and meet Eric at the RAC Club where his chauffeur-driven limousine waited to drive us to Croydon. I had not had much time to explain to Lars exactly who Eric was: there wasn't much to explain. I had forgotten, if I had bothered to find out during our previous fairly Bacchanalian week, how little we had in common: probably little more than an Australian passport. We found out much more on the drive to the airport. Eric sat between us. I had no chance to look at Lars. Eric regaled Lars with the account of our previous trip—the places we had been to—but was even more lyrical about the night ahead of us. He slapped my knee repeatedly in his excitement. This time he wanted to see all the sights—Les Folies Bergère, the Lido, a trip on the Bateaux Mouches—none of the recherché haunts David and I had led him to, enjoyable as they may have been. By the time we reached Croydon, we were worn out, and my knee was tender. Eric paid the driver, asked if he could wait with us in the car whilst he cleared airport papers for take-off, took his own bag into the Control Room with him, and left us staring dumbly after him.

'Can we stand it?' I asked Lars.

'Definitely not,' he said. Our bags were still in the car. We instructed the driver to turn round quickly and drive us straight back to London. I never saw Eric again, and I don't suppose he forgave us: nor can I see why he should have done.

Flying trips to Paris must have been our instinctive and most easily accessible response to the restraints still in force in post-war England. No one, in those days, thought of a quick trip to Amsterdam, Geneva, Brussels and certainly not the vast adventure of the Stratocruiser to the U.S. David occasionally went without me en route to visit his mother, now living in the South of France, and on these occasions I would try and meet him in Paris on his return trip. I had booked one such trip to coincide with Lars' return to Göteborg after he had been in London for a few days.

On the morning of Lars' departure, several dozen majestic red roses were delivered to me, with a loving note. I had time only to jam them into a bucket, still in their cellophane wrapping, before driving with Lars to the British Airways Terminal at Victoria. Then, no one drove to the airport: passengers bussed to Northolt Aerodrome from Victoria. We sat, holding hands, and weeping, side by side in the Departure Hall, waiting for his flight to be called. Farewells being an emotional business, Lars tenderly told me to go home rather than endure painful moments of waiting. I went, thankfully, as I had not much time to pack and go back to Victoria in order to catch my own flight to Paris.

It seemed a shame to leave the roses. I had never had such a magnificent bouquet in my life. I grabbed them as I left the apartment, dried my tears and patched up my smudged mascara and caught a taxi to Victoria. There I was to meet a girlfriend booked on the same flight who had invited David and me to spend the night in her apartment in Paris.

Lars was sitting where I had left him. He saw the roses first, my transformed and happy face next. I returned to my seat beside him. His flight was finally cancelled, just as mine was called.

At the check-in desk, a frantic Frenchman was pleading with the ticket clerk to get him on to the fully booked Paris flight. In those days, I think, there was only one per day. His wife was having a baby—now—that very minute. He had to be on that plane. I thrust my ticket into his hands, the roses into the arms of my puzzled friend, introduced them and asked her to explain to David when he met the flight that I had been unavoidably detained.

Sometime the following year Lars got a divorce. I was told that, Swedish fashion, I was officially named as the reason. I gathered it was rather like a job application when asked for references—you filled in a form, paid your fee, and got your freedom. But ties were loosening between us; and simultaneously four years of pressure from David's mother and the censure from some members of her side of the family were beginning to take their toll. I was considered not only a 'femme fatale', but from Australia to boot. I never met my critics; his father's relations, the Mountbattens, remained charming and friendly, from the time I had first spent a weekend visit to them—a weekend notable for the fact that Philip had driven over that afternoon to formally ask King George VI for the hand of his daughter in marriage and news of his reception was eagerly awaited, and for the fact that not a single fish was caught in one of the most famous stretches of trout river in southern England. I had been lent a rod and had tried my hand at it for the first time, frightening every fish for miles around.

In order to prepare for the royal wedding it was thought advisable that David move in with his grandmother, the grand-daughter of Queen Victoria, at Kensington Palace. So we gave up the lease of our Chelsea flat and our nights together. I crept, as silently as possible, up her back stairs to David's room in the servants' attics. Whilst waiting for the wedding, Prince Philip moved into an adjoining room.

A concern was how David was to afford an appropriate wedding present for the royal bride and groom, soon to go on display. One night, at a large dinner party, I sat next to a businessman who proudly told me that he was manufacturing what, in 1947, was a most revolutionary and expensive record player, to be called a Deccola. Until then, records did not slip automatically on top of one another when playing in sequence, which this magic machine would do. By the end of dinner, I had procured, free, for David, the very first off the production line and the manufacturer had procured valuable publicity as it went on prominent display with the royal wedding presents.

* * *

The fact that I could not, as a divorcee, accompany David to the Royal Enclosure at Ascot (even had I wished to) was but a tiny indication of the pinpricks suffered by David. We were not to know of the vast, ironic turntable awaiting those standards; but I was also having a wonderful time and, although in love, found the world full of amusement—a state I had found sadly lacking in marriage. But we had five happy years of love, fun and friendship—a friendship which lasted until David's death. My first marriage was by now happily forgotten, its consequences lingering, but life also lived long enough and well enough to recognise the blessings that fate had bestowed. I was saved, in all probability, by the Pope and the antiquated royal approval laws, respectively, from missing the joys to come later with my second marriage. David, understandably, got married to someone else (with the mistaken idea that she was very rich), leaving me with his dog, his car, and, just as we had parted in Australia years before, both of us in tears.

Shortly after drying mine I met Stanley Haynes. That liaison lasted for four years until I met my husband, and through him finally grow up, to look back with amazement at the creature I was in those years. Perhaps this is one of the things that growing up means. I cannot feel any shame or guilt at my behaviour, partly because I cannot believe that the creature was me. I am also incredibly glad that I felt none at the time, and was therefore able to enjoy life to the full without a thought to the future. I don't think I hurt anyone much and my chief regret is that I made nothing of any of the opportunities offered me to concentrate on a direction in life.

But, as four years of that other life were spent with Stanley, some residue of enrichment must remain, however traumatic its termination.

Stanley was a writer/film producer of self-taught erudition and culture, and through him I regained something of the influences of my childhood with my grandmother. He taught me to listen to music—to need music. Before I met him, I had existed without it except for Chula's concerts and occasional opera outings. He was one of the five men who had formed Cineguild, a unique grouping of complementary talents responsible for some of the better films of the 1940s in England—David Lean, Eric Ambler, Ronald Neame, Anthony Havelock-Allan, and Stanley between them writing, directing or producing. Stanley wrote and produced with David, *Oliver Twist* and *Great Expectations*. I was to become his fourth wife—something which horrified my grandmother but which my parents took in their stride. I suspect by this time they were relieved that I was about to settle down with someone—anyone, within reason. Over the four years, I hesitated, as I detected an inkling of why his last three marriages had not survived—largely to do with Stanley's moods, depressions, and, in my case, jealousy. Admittedly, the latter with just cause.

Stanley was in Fiji making a film when I met the man I was to marry, at someone else's engagement party. The hostess, Rada Penfold-Hyland, an Australian friend of my youth, took my hand and drew me across the room to a young man standing on his own.

'I want you two to meet,' she said, 'because you are the two nicest people I know.'

I had certainly done nothing to deserve that, but she was right about Emmet. We spent the next two hours talking together, and when the friends with whom I had arrived beckoned me away for dinner I knew I had met an exceptional soul and I also knew that we were in some way inextricably linked—by past lives, present life, or future lives I didn't know, but after our meeting brief fleeting flashes of his image would come into my mind, unbidden.

Apart from the journalism, and the film PR, over the years I continued to earn very small and spasmodic sums of money in a very desultory way: the incipient careers nipped in the bud either by the attractions of a man, or a journey—the two usually combined. Having exhausted the possibilities of Scandinavia, I fell upon the Rahvis sisters.

Rae and Dora Rahvis were larger-than-life sisters who cut a flamboyant swathe through London's fashion world. They operated from a large and elegant house in Upper Grosvenor Street: Rae lived on the top floor; workrooms below; mirrored and chandelier-decked salon on the grand first floor; and, as a new venture, a boutique ready-to-wear department on the ground floor.

I had a friend, Diana Strathcarron, who had been asked to manage this boutique. She enlisted me as her partner, neither of us knowing anything about salesmanship, the sewing on of a button or the shortening of a hem, but both in possession of a useful address book. We did well. Enjoyment was provided by frequent trips upstairs where we were privy to the spectacular rows between Dora, Rae, the seamstresses and, quite frequently, the clients. It was great fun.

I was expecting Stanley to be in Fiji for several months but the thought of any other romantic attachment did not occur. Only those odd flashes of memory of the young man with whom I'd spent two hours. Sitting in the dentist's chair one day, mouth agape, my dentist, both Australian and a font of gossip, said, 'You met that young Irish doctor of Rada's, Emmet Dalton? He has consulting rooms downstairs—such a splendid chap, and he's just discovered he has a potentially fatal heart condition—probably not long to live. He only found out when he went for a medical for National Service call-up.' Bruce went back to his drill and probe—my heart plummeted. I discovered more: Emmet had a rare heart deformity—a sub-aortic stenosis. Heart surgery was in its infancy. Perhaps it would improve in time to save him—perhaps not. I thought about him intermittently over the next six months, but short of having an attack of toothache, there was no way I could monitor his progress.

At the end of six months, Rada asked me to her wedding party. Stanley was still in Fiji. I did not particularly want to go, but, wondering if I might meet the doctor again, I went—arriving early, eyes constantly on the door. He wasn't there and my disappointment was intense. An old friend, Dick Austin, was, and so, having agreed to dine with him, and said our goodbyes, we headed for the front door. As it opened for us, Emmet walked in. I learnt later that he had not wanted to come either but he hurried through his last patient and made the effort in case I should be there.

Two minutes later and both our lives would have been different. I asked Dick to wait a few minutes: Emmet and I stood just inside the hallway. No time for preliminaries; he asked me to dine. No time to risk there being no second chance, I asked him to come to dinner with me the following night.

Wedding to John Spencer,
Sydney, October 1940

With wartime
fiancé US pilot
Joshua Barnes

At Elizabeth Bay,
Sydney, during
the war

With US fiancé Torbert
Macdonald, Sydney

With Swedish love Lars Schmidt, London, 1947

With David, Marquis of Milford Haven, at the Hotel du Reserve at Beaulieu, 1946

In London, 1947, with photographer George Silk, whom I had tentatively promised to marry

Wedding to Emmet Dalton, London, May 1953,
with photographer Baron Nahum and actress Kay Walsh

On holiday in Spain with Emmet and the children, 1957

Wedding to Bill
Fairchild, 1992

Reflecting
on life,
circa 2002

CHAPTER 12

I HAD settled into my first permanent home, no longer rented, but bought, decorated and furnished by myself—a lovely and romantic attic apartment in Mount Street looking down Berkeley Square—up ninety-two stairs. An added bonus was that Bill Gustav, the manager of the adjacent Connaught Hotel, kept a maid's attic bedroom permanently available for me on the nights (more than once) when I had arrived home without a door key. The stairs could not have helped Emmet's heart condition but, if it seriously worried him, he hid this from me. He was quietly spoken, handsome and intelligent, but inexperienced in what till then had been 'my' world of travel, and parties, and international 'society'. I, although I was unaware of it, was inexperienced in the 'real' world. Not so much inexperienced as unthinking. I had certainly encountered cruelty and kindness, good and evil, life and death, strength and weakness, purpose and aimlessness, but I had not given them more than a passing nod of acquaintance as I flitted through life, accepting opportunity. Here was a young man who not only recognised but lived with them all, choosing the positive side of life's coinage—he was kind, wise, full of purpose and was not afraid to confront life or his probable early death. Above all he was good, and strong, and—by some miracle chance, or perhaps upbringing harking back to memories of a role model in my grandfather, Sammie—I recognised this. I discovered that it is possible to grow up suddenly—to burst into adulthood—if you meet a twin soul whose strength beckons you into maturity.

He came to dinner. He had never been asked to dine by a girl. He still lived with his parents. He was a devout Catholic and like many young Irishmen had considered the priesthood before medicine. He was twenty-eight years old, three years younger than I. He was also, I was later to learn, a wonderful doctor.

That first night we talked for hours. He kissed me goodnight. I think within a week we were lovers. There was never a doubt in his mind that somehow we were to marry but the struggle with his religious beliefs and his aghast parents was a fierce one. For my part, I was content to wake up in the mornings, and with a silly grin on my face, hug myself with incredulous joy, repeating aloud to the empty room, 'He's so good! He's so good!' If this makes Emmet sound dull, pious or precious, it is my paucity of words. He had tremendous humour and tremendous understanding and love for people. I felt cocooned with care.

He tried to convince his parents that he was doing what he believed to be the right thing as well as it being what he wanted in life. He spent hours with the priest at Farm Street, with Monsignor Cashman, the papal nuncio in London, trying to find ways in which we could be married in his church. I offered to become a Catholic but he would not hear of it. It did not occur to me to wish John Spencer, the obstacle to a church wedding, dead, and we both rejected as spurious the possibility of applying for an annulment of my brief marriage. We were both conscious of time passing, of the precariousness of Emmet's future, of the probable years it might take to procure such an annulment and of the falsity of what securing it would entail. I would have had to declare my intention never to have children with John Spencer, and perhaps even ask him to co-operate in such a declaration. Fat chance.

While Emmet was struggling with his priests and his parents, I busied myself with the practical consideration of where we would live. I hated leaving my chic apartment but it made sense, along with turning our backs on the stairs, to find a house where Emmet could also run his medical practice. We had just settled on an intriguing, tall sliver of a house behind what is now the Hilton Hotel—it had the narrowest frontage in London, with just enough width for the entrance on ground level and one window above the front door for each of the rooms above, widening to normal proportions at the rear mews—when chance dumped a package in our laps.

Friends Diana and David Strathcarron were also looking for more space and had found an imposing end-of-terrace house in Albion Street, overlooking the north side of Hyde Park. The area had become the happy hunting ground of prostitutes during the war and being Crown Land the Church Commissioners, who were the freeholders, were looking for tenants to bring the area back into its earlier repute. The houses, four storeys high, formed a perfect late Regency Terrace and the recessed doorways and basement steps formed a perfect backdrop for vertical sex. Every morning almost every doorway was littered with discarded condoms. The interiors had not been architecturally tampered with. The commissioners hoped to attract respectable tenants who would both redecorate the interiors and sweep the ladies off the doorsteps. Competition was high and rents were low: the priority of the landlords was the desirability of lessees.

Diana had managed to get herself and David onto the top of the list, as a lord would have been a great kick-off to set the tone for the rest of the street. Sadly, this particular lord was having a temporary cash flow problem and so they reluctantly decided they couldn't afford the house and passed it on to us. We had no title, but a solid professional occupation. I was on the commissioners' doorstep before the doors opened the following morning and we won the twenty-six-year lease on the understanding that we would take on both the restoration of the house and the banishment of the girls.

I said goodbye to the jolly Rahvis sisters and my jolly job, and five months after our meeting at Rada's wedding Emmet and I were married.

Religious prejudices overshadowed our wedding as they had overshadowed the wedding of my parents. My husband left his home and his weeping Catholic mother and unspeaking Catholic father at 9 a.m. one morning to meet his divorced Presbyterian future wife at Caxton Hall. Baron gave me away: he approved of my marriage. Darling Baron, who would be dead at fifty, was particularly a life enhancer—but my nearest and dearest all tend to die young. An American friend, Blevins Davis, lent us his new Rolls Royce for our wedding journey, along with his chauffeur fresh from the Queen's employment, and therefore a flourishing English feather for an American cap.

Chula and Lisba had asked us to spend our brief weekend honeymoon with them in Cornwall, and so we set off for three days in which two events occurred which were to influence the next five years of my life, as well as changing it forever.

First, we were convinced our daughter Lisa was conceived in Cornwall on our wedding night. Then, the next day Chula put to Emmet a question which started me on the road to being, for want of a more exact terminology, a Thai spy. A pregnant Thai spy. 'Would you object to Robin having a job?' was the question.

* * *

Chula's request was occasioned by an approach to him from his own government for advice. Public relations had never been a particular concern of the Thai embassy and therefore there had never been the post of press attaché. But now some Thai newspapers were printing garbled versions of reports carried by responsible English newspapers that emphasised the poverty of the North East province of Thailand. This poverty was actually relative and localised and the reports were exaggerated; but the Thai reports carried with them editorial comments stressing that the English, supposed friends and allies, wrote disparagingly of the poverty and primitive conditions of Thailand, and the inefficiency and corruption of the Thai Government. The inference was 'Look! These are our friends and see what they print about us in their leading newspapers.'

It was fodder for Communist propaganda, then a tiny stirring in Thailand and taken seriously only by a few, Chula amongst them. Champagne communists amid the Western educated upper class intellectuals were a breed which in those days, in South East Asia in the 1950s, seemed far-fetched indeed. The stories were gathered by reputable English journalists in the bars and at the cocktail parties of the grander hotels and embassies, and printed in good faith in the more serious English newspapers. Not one of these newspaper men in Bangkok spoke Thai, to my knowledge, and very few of them had close Thai friends except amongst the old Oxbridge, Etonian, Harrovian Thais whom they met at the smart international gatherings. What was needed was someone to influence the British press lords at a fairly high level, and so the government came to Chula. Chula, intensely practical, saw that a Thai national would never understand the British press mentality sufficiently and that few English people knew both enough high ranking British journalists or newspaper proprietors and enough of the Thai nature; but, if a person could be found who had these two qualifications and was not even English, so much the better.

There I was: it seemed to him an inspired chance. I was Australian: I was not tainted with preconceived prejudice, or precious little knowledge. I had many influential friends in the press. I had just married an Irishman, a national of a country who would understand the plight of a small country (this he told me later). Of course I said 'yes' at once. At first I thought only of lovely tax-free wine and minor diplomatic privileges, with no intimation that this was the beginning of a five-year love affair with Thailand and the Thai people, which would end only with the death of my husband and the almost simultaneous defection of my immediate boss, General Phao, with £3 million of the country's money, to Geneva (where he eventually shot himself).

I was allowed to work from home, sharing Emmet's secretary and only occasionally going into the embassy in Ashburn Place. I already knew Prince Wongsa, the Ambassador and his wife, aunt of the young Queen Sirikit of Thailand, who was later to open the first Thai restaurant in Bangkok (I rather think this may have been the first in the world).

To begin with, I, carefully tutored by Chula, wrote earnest letters to the *Times* and the *Guardian* and met with South East

Asia experts at the *Economist* and the like in the cheery belief that I, too, seemed expert. I was assumed by them to be so, I imagine, or I must have seemed an odd choice to these learned chaps, especially as I became increasingly and obviously pregnant. But my borrowed view was an inside one, an infinitely wise one, a royal one tinged with the history and culture of the Thai people, not gleaned in the bar of the Oriental Hotel by all the stringers of the papers who knew the political personages and were self-appointed experts.

With hindsight I wonder which was the true view, and how valid and objective such truths can ever be. I believed in the basic innocence of the people. Now, over fifty years later, I learn from one of these bar-room specialists that my lovable General Phao, my genial boss, was chief of the entire opium trade, with a few minor businesses like prostitution on the side. This, though, still emerges from the memory of his benign despotism as a sort of innocence, or, at least, a naiveté, his as well as mine. Three million pounds and the entire opium trade can never be termed petty corruption, and it was this corruption which he loudly disclaimed on behalf of himself and the cabinet, while pressing crisp hundred-dollar bills into my palm whenever we met.

He was a big man. Not only for a Thai, but by any standards; with a smiling face and shining white hair, and an outgoing manner. We first met in London when I had officially been press officer at the Thai embassy in London for over a year. On that occasion, he came with Chula and Lisba to lunch, and invited me and Emmet to Thailand. Lisa was eleven months old when we left, in separate aeroplanes, which caution, I suspect, was the seed of my ever-after fear of flying.

General Phao was not only Chief of Police—the most powerful post in the country—but Deputy Prime Minister, Chief of Intelligence, and, rather conveniently, Finance Minister. In Bangkok, we were met both by emissaries of the government and family retainers of Chula. We stayed in Chula's house; called a palace, but in reality a large, cool and comfortable villa by the river with a waterside pavilion. We slept under vast, tented mosquito nets, and, before air-conditioning, were wafted off to sleep by the gentle whirr of the ceiling fans. In the mornings, the smiling servants wheeled in a trolley of exquisite exotic fruits to my beside, followed by my personal contact, General Phao's aide de camp, Lieutenant Thana, with a list of the day's appointments.

General Phao and I got on exceedingly well together. The Prime Minister, Pibul, in addition to not being my immediate boss, had a less sunny and outgoing personality. Whilst the pattern of my work brought me closer to Phao, protocol linked me with Pibul whenever he was in England or I was in Thailand, and, in addition to the formal audiences over small cups of tea or coffee, there were official farewells on leave taking. These were the occasions for a clasped handshake, rather than the traditional Thai greeting of palms pressed together in prayer-like salute. The handshakes were the opportunity for Pibul to pass over his own fistful of dollars, as distinct from Phao's. I never was able to count them until safely in private, and I never was able to thank him, as thanks are considered bad form by the

Thais. The pleasure is, rightly, in the giving. In our case, there was considerable pleasure in the receiving, and puzzlement as to the exact nature of the gift. Was it a gift, or payment? I was paid, although not very much, by the London embassy, and the amounts in cash were not only arbitrary in their varying size but spasmodic in occurrence. Once, an ADC murmured, as I left Pibul, something about my expenses, and so, to my conscience, expenses they became. Payment would have made me uneasy in the face of the taxation authorities: a gift, unacknowledged, uneasy in the face of my western upbringing.

We saw Thailand under perfect conditions. It was the cool season. We lived in the most comfortable house in Bangkok. We ate the most delicious food imaginable. In those days, indigenous Thai restaurants were virtually unknown: Thai cooking was done by Thai servants in private houses; if you wished to go to a restaurant the cook was Chinese, undeniably good Chinese, but not authentic Thai. As we seldom went to a restaurant, our various hosts vied with each other in providing banquets, but the best cook of all was Chula's.

* * *

We spent a week at Chula's seaside residence at Hua-Hin—I terrified of the spiders and Emmet of the snakes. The spiders, the size of small crabs in fur coats, scuttled across the floor, burrowed their way under our mosquito net, and went into battle formation. We crouched on the bed trying to count their legs. Seven legs were relatively harmless—eight meant instant death. I may have forgotten exact numerals but not the panic of trying to count. The snakes were chiefly in Emmet's imagination and nightmares, and occasioned by visits to Snake Farm coupled with folk memory of Saint Patrick.

The Prime Minister, General Phao, and the members of the cabinet held a splendid dinner party in my honour in Manankasila House, the Thai equivalent of London's Lancaster House. Emmet and I were the only outsiders present. In Thailand I felt like a large white slug amidst the fluttering, exquisite, Thai women and my voice boomed loud and coarse in my ears, particularly as no one else spoke at dinner, not one of the seventeen other women. We arrived to a battery of arc lights and popping bulbs and an army of photographers; all of whom disappeared about halfway through dinner. At the end, we were ushered through a courtyard into a private theatre where the Royal Thai Ballet performed a ballet especially for me. The music was played on the ancient classical Thai instruments and the dancers posed and undulated in their superb costumes singing what to me then were incomprehensible sounds. Unmistakably, however, I heard 'Mrs Robin Da-a-a-altun'. The beaming faces of my hosts confirmed it. The music and the song, like the ballet, had been composed for me: the words were presented to me on a printed sheet, and when translated read 'Oh, Mrs Robin Dalton, the Intelligent One, we salute you'. At that moment I knew that as soon as I could I must learn to speak Thai.

The Prime Minister, General Pibul, asked if there was

anything else I would like so I asked if the song could be recorded for me. I had my record two days later and on the flip side the Thai boxing music—a wonderfully stirring rhythm to which the contestants bash each other to bits, having first prayed that they may do just that.

After interval and coffee, the lights went out again, a screen came down, and I discovered where all the photographers had gone halfway through dinner. They had gone to a dark room and some few hours later I saw the film of our arrival at the dinner. I have the record and the film—one scratched and the other battered—or I would not be believed, or myself believe, that these things had ever happened to me.

Everything we saw was presented under the best possible conditions, although this is not to say that they were false conditions. To visit the river market or the temple at Ayudhya up river, I had my own police launch to transport me. The temples were visited in the cool of the day with few other sightseers. When we visited the self-help settlements of which the government was justly proud, our guide was the director general of the region, and a former Miss Thailand showed us round a northern jungle village. We had the best ringside seats at the Thai boxing match and we were helped on to the broad backs of the gentlest elephants. I asked if we might visit Chiang Mai (long before any tourists had heard of it) on the northern border of the Shan States, by train, so that we might see something of the country. I did not realise that this simple request would result in my own train, but by the next day I had my private train, searchlights mounted on the roof, with my very own guard of honour to fare-well us and my personal bodyguard of thirty soldiers, armed with tommy guns. I remember I gave the American ambassador, Jack Peurifoy, a lift—probably putting a curse on the poor man, who was killed in a road accident the following week. In Chiang Mai we stayed in a newly built palatial villa owned by the richest Chinese merchant in the province (opium-funded, I expect), and my thirty soldiers paraded up and down outside my windows.

The mayor was to give a dinner party in my honour on the night of our arrival. I arrived feeling distinctly ill: the doctor from the local hospital came and dysentery was diagnosed.

After a week, I was well enough to get up but Emmet had to return to England, and our old friend, Steven Runciman, flew out to spend the remainder of the trip with me. The mayor's dinner party at which I had never appeared became a farewell luncheon instead.

We were twelve at table, Steven and I being the only Europeans, and the place on my right was reserved for Dr Rabieb who had looked after me so well during my week in bed. The mayor explained that he was always very busy at his hospital and that we must excuse him if he was a little late. Soon, however, the doctor arrived and, smiling and bowing, we all exchanged greetings, heads turning politely and attentively to listen.

'And, Mrs Dalton, how are you?'

'Much better, thank you.'

'And your motions—how are they?'

'They are very well too.'

Many smiles and approving nods around the table...

'And your period—has it come yet?'

An almost audible sigh of satisfaction greeted my answer that it had indeed, with no mishap.

We flew back to Bangkok in an aeroplane rattling with decrepitude and landed at Ayudhya in stifling heat to offload one passenger with a small briefcase and take on another two with many large cases and a dog in a crate. We stood panting under the wing as these two argued in increasing fury with the pilot. The shouts and curses and shaking fists eventually abated and the troupe climbed aboard amid shrugs from the crew.

'What was the problem?' I asked a neighbour as we settled for take-off.

'The pilot did not want to take them, as we are already very overweight,' I was told.

I flew back to England from Bangkok but not before General Phao had extracted from me a promise to return in six weeks in order to organise press and public relations for the first SEATO Conference, in 1955. Meticulously correct, he had already telephoned Emmet in London for his permission. So I had six weeks in which to be re-united with our baby daughter before flying out again. Although most of my time was taken up with entertaining, on dance floors and in bars, the foreign press, I had occasion to chat with the delegates and assess their degree of satisfaction with the arrangements, seating and sleeping. General Phao's attention to detail, passed on to his subordinates, equalled that of a great hostess or the most meticulously trained butler. A fresh toothbrush and a selection of toothpastes awaited each of his political guests, clean pyjamas were laid out in each room in case they had been forgotten, and, of course, a selection of beautiful gifts—boxed silver cufflinks, exquisite fans, and, for the few women or the wives back home, a length or two of superb Thai silk without which no Thai visitor ever departed, awaited in each suite. Eden was then Prime Minister, representing Great Britain. He did not appear to be a man ever to forget his toothbrush or his pyjamas and I did not dare voice more than a general query as to his comfort.

CHAPTER 13

ALL THROUGH the years of working for the Thai Government, and revelling in the experience of motherhood, I had the joy of seeing Emmet build a reputation for being the splendid doctor he was and, not unlike my childhood experience with my father, sharing in some part of his professional life. We had had time to enjoy our beautiful house, clean the girls off the front steps, and engage the first of a series of servants whose eccentricities were to mimic, but never to surpass, those of my parents' household.

Diary never kept after the disastrous publication of my teenage romanticisms, I nevertheless started, upon marriage, to keep a menu book—far more useful. I not only can remember the guests but the food and the wine (a sharp pang of regret when I contemplate the wine). Still limited by rationing, clothing and petrol had slid off first. Eggs, butter and cream followed. Not until 1954 were we able to discard the black market butcher and the horse meat steaks in French restaurants. During clothes rationing, Great Aunt Juliet's heavy tasselled and fringed white linen guest towels had been blithely chopped up to provide nappies for a friend's new baby, and I marked in the book the celebratory fillet steak on the night meat came off the ration— July, 1954.

We had celebrated our first week in the house by acquiring a butler and cook, Mr and Mrs Hawkins, who, we were to discover almost immediately, fitted into the pattern of married couples as staff, recognised—but not soon enough by us— universally. A bad egg almost always shares a nest with a good egg.

On their first night in attendance, Mrs Hawkins cooked us an impressive dinner. Hawkins was impressive in every respect. Resplendent in white jacket and gloves, he held out my chair in the candle-lit dining room, silver gleaming, fire softly glowing, napkins stiffly awaiting, wine impeccably poured. We left the house walking on air, preceded by Hawkins, car door opened with a bow and a flourish. On our arrival home, Hawkins, who must have had his nose pressed to the window, flew out the front door, and, with another bow and another flourish, ushered us inside. What bliss to find curtains drawn, lights lit, bed turned down, night attire waisted and reposing invitingly on our bed.

The following night we went in to dinner with happy anticipation. Candles were still lit. The wine splashed a little. The dinner was fine, Hawkins not quite so solicitous, and something amiss with his tie. Halfway through the second course, a tieless and jacketless figure lurched through the door.

'Mrs H says,' it bellowed at us, somewhat belligerently, 'do you want any more veg?'

The next morning, as I dried Mrs H's tears and studiously ignored the snores coming from their bedroom, I learned we were not the first of their employers to have enjoyed such a brief period of euphoria. Mr H was the bad egg. They left that day, Mrs H in tears, Mr H shouting abuse, kicking aside the empty bottles—ours—cluttering their bedroom floor.

Shortly after this, by whatever telephonic grapevine I have forgotten, I managed to trace splendid, funny and fondly remembered Nancy—mad, Scottish Nancy—who in my parents' house had so memorably lightened my Australian youth and had given my father such magnificent excuses for tease.

She was thrilled to hear from me, caught the train from Scotland at once—it did not occur to me to question the oddity of her, the perfect servant, being so immediately available—and re-entered my life. The house sparkled. I was cosseted. Emmet's suits were pressed and his shoes shone. Telephones were answered. Bliss again.

One day Nancy appeared blushing furiously and near to tears. She thrust a package into my hands. It had come through the post, addressed to her. Inside was a condom—used. We had just managed to clear most of them, along with the girls, off our front steps in the mornings, so it could not have been the first Nancy had ever seen, but this one had been directed, addressed, aimed at her.

The nice police inspector who came at our request gently questioned Nancy in Emmet's surgery: was it possible that she had any local acquaintance who could have done such a dastardly deed? Nancy blushed more furiously and rushed from the room. I felt dreadfully for her and was about to follow and comfort when I saw the policeman and my husband exchange looks.

'Do you agree with me, doctor?'

''Fraid so,' said Emmet, 'but thank you very much for coming.'

Patiently, he explained to me that he and the police officer had come to the same conclusion: Nancy had posted it to herself, having first scooped it up with the early morning's cleaning.

Nancy's psychosis (for such it was) escalated with alarming rapidity, triggered by my first confinement. Whilst I was in hospital giving birth, Nancy sang around the house, and took to wearing lipstick. On my return, she was as caring as ever, keeping me in bed for several days and pampering me with meals on trays. When I got up to dress for the first time, I discovered the shelf on which I kept my underwear empty.

'How sweet of Nancy,' I thought, 'and how unnecessary. She has washed all my underclothes.'

But, no, Nancy's blank incomprehension mirrored the blank shelves. I had nothing to wear.

Emmet began to ask me what I had done with his underpants.

We had an old-fashioned coke boiler in our basement. Brassiere straps and scraps of linen were amongst the debris he discovered in the embers one morning. Mine. His, however, were discovered, unwashed, under Nancy's pillow.

We were driven to the lengths of bed-searching by a chance entry by Emmet into her bedroom. Lamps were disconnected and shoved under the bed. Looking glasses were pasted over with newspaper.

It was evident that Nancy thought evil rays were directed at her through lamp and mirror. A classic symptom, it seemed. But she was wonderful with the baby. And wonderful as always in every other way. A harmless lunacy seemed a small price to pay. Underwear was reasonably expendable.

Sadly, it came to an abrupt end the day she told our daily cleaner that I was trying to poison the baby. Next step, Emmet told me, would be that she would poison the baby. By that night, all of us in tears, Nancy was packed off—to a nursing home— protesting and furious, but safe. All of us.

The Hawkins, and then Nancy, were to prove the first indication that I, like my mother, would attract eccentric servants. Nancy had never seemed unusual to me in the lexicon of servants of my childhood, all of them delightfully dotty.

CHAPTER 14

MY SECOND pregnancy coincided with stage two of my crash course in the Thai language bravely begun at the School of Oriental and African Studies at London University. The bravery was not on my part but on the part of the university and, above all, our teacher. Hardly anybody spoke Thai in London in those days and I think Stuart Symmonds was the only person who taught it. He had devised his method whilst in prison camp during the war, perfected it on his fellow prisoners, and was now facing his first five pupils at the university.

I was the only female in our ill-assorted group, which became glaringly more so as the weeks went by. My four companions were Victor Sassoon, of the Sassoon family, who wanted to learn Thai in order to live in Bangkok and teach English at the University there; a Scottish missionary who was being sent by his Wesleyan Ministry to the lovely hill villages of the beautiful Shan States borders to convert the happy peasants from their satisfying Buddhism to a dour Scots guilt (as no one in our class could understand what he was saying in English we were unable to gauge his progress in Thai); a car salesman from the Midlands who was being sent into the jungle to sell Land Rovers, presumably to replace elephants; and I have forgotten the identity of the fourth.

A small dusty room had been allocated to us in a narrow house in Torrington Square. After signing in in the main office of the University we had no more contact with anyone except our group, locked together in our little world of 'Oooos' and 'Aeees' and squealing grunts.

Once we had learnt to make the sounds to the symbols of the twenty-six consonants and the thirteen and a half (thirteen and a half will give an idea of the complexity...) vowels we left stage one. The system Stuart had devised was then, in 1956, a tremendous innovation. In order to teach us a totally new concept of language, in terms of alphabet and sounds, we had first to unlearn our own. We learnt phonetically, as children learn their first language, mouthing sounds to coincide with symbols on a blackboard. The sounds, coming from our assorted throats, were fairly horrid, but the symbols, written on the board and then into our notebooks, were beautiful. I loved the flowing symmetry to them. In the afternoons we listened to tapes and at night we did our homework and enlarged our vocabularies. My stomach grew in tandem with my stock of Thai words, and I am fairly sure that I was the only pregnant student at London University.

When the course finished and the other four dispersed to their various jobs, I continued with daily lessons at home from the wife of the First Secretary at the embassy. My small red exercise book now looks both beautiful and bewildering to me—the Thai characters beautiful, their meaning obscure. I have written the English translation beneath each line and am fascinated by the strange phrases on which I concentrated: I expect the car salesman's efforts revolved around carburettors and spark plugs, miles per gallon and four-wheel drive, whilst I was laboriously searching for the tactful translation of 'coup d'etat'.

* * *

Some months after I had graduated from SOAS, given birth to my second child, and was established as a recognised feature at the Embassy, I was invited by the editor of a London daily newspaper for drinks to meet his good friend from the Foreign Office. He had been, my friend explained, in the South East Asian section and stationed in Bangkok, which he had loved and sorely missed. He wanted an opportunity to talk over old times, old faces, old places, and, having heard about me, would love to meet me for just such a chat. Emmet and I went to drinks where, in a room containing no more than a dozen people, the chap from the Foreign Office managed to avoid me entirely. I thought it odd, however, that he appeared to spend all of his time with my husband. On the way home Emmet told me that on departure he had said how disappointed he'd been not to have had a chance to talk to me, and had, in fact, made such an issue of this that Emmet had invited him for a drink with us the following week. He felt he had somehow been pushed into it and had the distinct impression that Mr 'O' wished to see me alone.

Emmet obliged. He was busy with a patient and I poured drinks for our guest and waited for the mutual nostalgia. There was, however, no nostalgia and no preamble. The ice had barely been put in his drink when he broke his own ice and made his approach. It took me about fifteen years to learn that it was neither quite as blunt nor as clumsy as it then seemed.

The Foreign Office, he told me, had had their eye on me for some time. They were extremely impressed by the extent to which I had infiltrated the Thai Cabinet and by the trust and regard in which General Phao, in particular, seemed to hold me. They were well aware that I was the only 'farang' (foreigner) ever to have become close to General Phao, and they, the FO, would dearly love to take advantage of this. They needed a favour from the Thai Government—a favour which could not be requested through the normal diplomatic channels. I seemed the perfect—indeed the only—route through which they could operate.

Mr O barely gulped a sip from his drink before elaborating. I had not read many spy thrillers but I had seen a lot of movies and it seemed to me that this particular scenario was straight out of the rejected script department of a motion picture company. There languished in a Thai gaol a man who had fought on the wrong side in the war (as Thailand hadn't fought at all this confused me somewhat). The Thais did not want him there—he was, in fact, an embarrassment—but they also did not want him at liberty in Thailand. There was no conventional political excuse the British Government could provide to request his release, as he was a Thai national, but the British Government badly wanted him out. The man wanted to come to Britain. Names were mentioned: Pridi, the Thai wartime leader, now in exile, and Lord Mountbatten, who seemingly also wanted his release very badly. A British submarine would rendezvous by night at an arranged part of the coast and take him aboard. The British Government would privately give an undertaking that he would never be seen in Thailand again. My task would be to propose this scheme to General Phao and to Pibul, thus relieving everyone of any possible embarrassment, and, if it were approved, I would finalise the arrangements.

The story came to an end as abruptly as it had begun. He stared at me. I stared back—mouth, I expect, if not open, distinctly ajar. I realised that I had been asked a question: would I, or wouldn't I?

'I'll have to ask my husband,' I said.

Poor Mr O, I now realise could not have been prepared for what was to me then a perfectly normal response. Over the years, pieces of sense have slotted into the jigsaw of nonsense and it finally dawned on me that I was being vetted—and hopefully recruited—for British Intelligence. They had not bargained for a spy who had to ask her husband what to do. He put a very brave face on it, made an appointment to telephone me the next day, and extracted from me the promise that, apart from my husband, I would tell no one of our conversation, the man in the Thai gaol or the hovering submarine. I did wonder briefly what would happen to them both, but, after giving him my refusal next day I put the incident, if not out of mind, at least in a far back pocket marked 'secret'.

The decision to refuse was quickly reached.

'Don't be ridiculous,' said Emmet. 'You can't work for two masters and you have a perfectly straightforward and aboveboard job with the Thai Government, who are friendly to Britain, and you cannot possibly muddy that by working for someone else.'

The puzzle resolved itself slowly. When I no longer worked for them, I told Chula one day. 'You did right,' he said. 'If you had approached General Phao that would have been the end of your job. He never would have trusted you again.' About the man in gaol and the Foreign Office he voiced no opinion: he was interested only in the personal relationship between me and my employers which could so easily have been wrecked.

A year or two later I ran across two old friends in the space of a few months. One, Dick Austin, had been First Secretary at the Australian embassy in Tokyo at the time and had been asked by his government, on behalf of the British Government, what, if anything, he knew of me. As we had had an intense romantic attachment some years previously, discretion wrestled with quite a fund of knowledge, but curiosity was uppermost in his mind as to what I could possibly have been up to. Nothing he could have told them had, however, put them off their approach. I imagine he made me sound like a girl who did not have to ask her husband.

The other friend, Fergus MacCaddie, was the then Commander in Chief of Australian Military Forces in South East Asia, stationed in Malaysia. He and Dick were given bulky dossiers on me and my movements since I had come to England and were asked to fill in details of my youth. The information they gleaned from my dossier saved me years of filling them in on gossip when I finally met them, individually, again.

Then, some ten years later, with Chula, General Phao and Emmet all dead, I was at a dinner party in London and seated next to a man working in the South East Asia section of the Foreign Office. He had known Mr O, who was then retired. As conversation was flagging and as over ten years seemed long enough to keep a secret, and as, in a sense, it was his secret I was giving back into his safe keeping, I told him the tale and my opinion that the Foreign Office were incredibly clumsy. I could, I said, so easily have given the whole thing away and blown, metaphorically, the submarine right out of the water—the man condemned to imprisonment for ever.

He gazed at me with amazement that someone so naive could ever have been seriously considered for any undertaking, however trivial. He told me the facts of espionage life. There had quite obviously never been a man in gaol, a submarine or any wish that I should approach the Thai Government on any pretext. I was simply being vetted as a candidate for recruitment by the British, and their decision as to whether to take their approach one step further depended on my answer. I had been proven a dud. I have occasionally regretted it.

The final elementary lesson I learned over lunch not long ago with an ex-MI5 officer, now retired, who was also once a friend of Chula's. I had continued to puzzle over the circuitous route by which Mr O talked to me. We had been together at a party at his instigation and he had ignored me. Why had he concentrated on my husband at that first meeting? My old friend patiently explained that my background, home life, personal relationships and general financial stability were important factors. I had probably been photographed at the party. My husband and house had been scrutinised. I had passed all the tests except the final ones: I believed everything I was told; and I did everything my husband told me.

CHAPTER 15

WITH A second marriage I had learnt the meaning of respect. True and enduring love was there, and sex, but both were pathways to the rock of respect. Experiencing it for the first time in my love life I recognised its impact. It meant I did nothing of which my gentle husband might have disapproved. This would have seemed a betrayal of his love. Without effort, miraculously, I believe I became a better person, blessed with jolly memories of a discarded life, viewed now through a happy, albeit astonished haze.

I was four months pregnant with our second child when my husband first became seriously ill, the first indication being coughing up blood. For four weeks the doctors didn't think it was his damaged heart, but lung cancer. Lung cancer at thirty-two didn't seem fair or right, not when we'd accepted the heart deformity. The tests would tell, and while waiting I had only to weather the sympathetic predictions of Irish Mary, my daily.

'How's Doctor?' she would say, and one day, when we'd been told to wait another twenty-four hours for results, I said, 'I'm afraid he's very ill, Mary.'

'Oh, dear,' she said, 'Isn't it always the same, Mrs Dalton. It's always the nice quiet ones who go first.'

The tests were negative and we had another year and a half in which Emmet was able to see his son born before we discovered it was his heart after all, and Mary was able to have her laments in company.

Memory's own selector button operates at random. Now, when I think of my husband's last night with me it is a vivid picture I receive each time of shaving his back before his operation. And going back twice, memories through memories, I remember that while shaving him, that smooth, muscular and broad back, I remembered back to the night we had first loved each other. The fire in my bedroom was alight and when he undressed and walked away from me across the room I was surprised and pleased and somehow proud to see the same back, not fully discerned in its perfect symmetry and strength under his clothes. I had loved him already, but this physical beauty of body was an unexpected gift he had brought me which I had not needed. Now, in shaving him, I hated to scrape off the few downy hairs and I thrust from my mind the vision of the scar which would soon mar it. A scythe cutting his body in two; heart surgery was in its infancy—keyhole surgery long in the future. We chatted a little about practical things—money, who would help financially if he should die, as we had never saved money. He said, 'I don't worry about you. If you have been able to live through the last five years with this constant dread hanging over you in the way you have, you will be able to cope with whatever life has to offer in the future.'

I held his hand, his strong gentle hand. There really wasn't anything to say—goodnight, perhaps, a message to his father who had never fully come to terms with our marriage. 'Tell him I don't hold his attitude against him. I understand. I know he loves me. He can't help it.' I don't remember. The things I remember are his back when I shaved it; his words which entered my very blood like a transfusion of strength; his hand as I took it, so like my son's now. And, then, when he had said goodnight, his back again as he walked away from me down the hospital corridor to the bathroom in the new blue dressing gown his father had given him in advance for his birthday. It was the first of December: his birthday—his thirty-fourth—was not for another ten days but there might not be need for a present by that time. I had already bought, too, our daughter's Christmas present, her first tricycle, so that he could share in the buying of it and by Christmas, if he should be dead, the present would not be such a lonely one. Our son, at fourteen months, would not be aware of Christmas yet.

His sister slept in the house that night so that I should not be alone during the long, long hours of the operation in the morning. But, in the morning, I could not stay in the house and thought for something to do, somewhere to go, that would match the effort he was making and would bring me close to him in our joint wish to live. His God, in whom I had never fully or consciously believed, was perhaps just a refuge in a vast world of concept where I could call on his beliefs, and perhaps because I was a part of him they would come to help me. I chose St James' Church in Spanish Place—never Emmet's church, or one to which to my knowledge, he had ever been. Perhaps I wanted it to be my own choice or perhaps it was because I could buy food for lunch in the High Street around the corner. I don't remember the idea of the food, only that the children and their nanny and my sister-in-law were in the house and I must, through all this time, have been buying food and cooking it. I do not remember neglecting this necessity.

The church was not empty. There were a few housewives like myself, an old woman or two, dusty pale sunlight mingling with the candles, and two cleaning women with straw brooms. I sat on the edge of a pew, an intruder, borrowing my place. I could not presume on the God, the force, the whatever great strength in which I did not believe to intervene and interrupt the flow of anything so basic as Emmet's life or death because of my own puny needs. Also, perhaps there was some superstition, a feeling that it was tempting the benevolence of this fate to ask for something not in its power to bestow. No: I must ask for something which required an equal effort from me and which I myself could provide if nothing and no one came to help me. He was called God, this force in whom Emmet believed, so, 'Please God,' I prayed, 'give me the strength to bear whatever is in store for us. Just let me bear it.'

I stayed until the time came when the doctors had said they could telephone and then I went home. Emmet's sister came to the door: she was smiling. 'It's all right—he's all right—it's all over.' Then I cried—oh, how I cried; and dried my eyes and she patted my shoulders and we went upstairs and the telephone started to ring.

The nice young house doctor rang and said I might come to see Emmet in the afternoon although he would be in great pain and would not be very aware of my presence. 'But it helps,' he said, 'It helps, just if you sit and hold his hand.' Oh, why was I frightened. Now, when I remember that I was frightened the thought is a sharp pain that I did not give him as much help as I might have done. His sister offered to come with me, and I needed her. I had been warned of the oxygen tent in which I would find him, and the blood drip on one side and the tubes from his wound draining on the other side, and I was afraid to face it alone. Nobody had warned me of his pain—of how his face would look black and grey with pain and drained of all blood and the usual tints of flesh. I held his hand but all he could say to me, if indeed he knew it was me, was, 'Take away the pain—oh, please take away the pain.' The pain was between us; it made a mockery of his strength and struck him down to the level of ordinary men. It jeered at the bond between us which in full consciousness would have restored the personality of my husband to that black and grey face on the pillow. Every two minutes they took his pulse. The doctors had told me that if his pulse rate remained stable he could leave the oxygen tent in twenty-four hours and we could begin to look forward rather than back. In each two-minute interval hung our lives.

Then—a blank—a long gap in my memory. Only now, as I write this, over the years of that blank, do I remember that Tam and Maggy Williams bundled me off to a celebratory dinner at the Ivy. We laughed and cried and joked and I was swept along by their love and the shared enjoyment of our lives—theirs, mine, Emmet's. Champagne had never seemed so effervescent. At lunchtime the next day Emmet's old doctor came with more champagne. We drank and celebrated and I think I cried a little more. I remember the chimney piece and resting my head on my hand on it and sobbing, 'Oh, George, I love him so much.'

'I know you do, old girl. I know you do.'

But was it that day or another day—a day when he was already dead and I cried, 'I loved him so much'? The events are mixed in the mind: the memory of the carvings on the chimney piece is vivid—and the words and old George's sympathetic murmurings, but whether Emmet was dead or alive then, this I do not remember.

That afternoon when I visited him the oxygen tent was gone. Emmet was still grey, with a stubble of unshaven whisker on his face which looked indecent, as if purposefully left there to emphasise his pain and his helplessness. But he was better and in control once more, as always. He was very proud of his pulse rate and made me feel it. He had never had a normal one before and was delighted at this novelty. He was able to tell me all the details of his operation and how very much worse his condition had been than they had suspected, and how marvellously the surgeon had displayed his skill.

'Are you happy?' he asked when he had finished. I could not say yes because I knew we had only won the first small victory.

'I feel as if I have just run a very long race,' was the best I could do.

'I love you,' he said. I didn't tell him I loved him too. I didn't say it. I don't know why. It seemed unnecessary to me, but for him to have used up his new little strength to say it to me may have meant that it was necessary to him, and in this I failed him. He asked for orange juice, and although there was a greengrocer across the street and I could have gone, it was late and foggy and past the children's bedtime and I needed to get home to them. 'I'll bring it with me later—around 7.30—will that be all right?'

I never told him that last time that I loved him and I never got him his orange juice, for by the time I got back to the hospital that night he had already started on the road to dying and the oranges lay forgotten forever on a waiting-room table.

Then sharp into my memory springs the window pane in that waiting room. It was solid—an inescapable and tangible hard surface on which to concentrate as the ground beneath my feet became a void. It reflected me; and it was hard and cold and therefore a necessity to accept. I looked through it to the fog, and felt it and pressed my hands against it and talked to it. I told it he was dying, that this was what I had prepared for and it had come and I was standing up looking out a window into a fog with a white ceiling light reflected behind me and my husband was dying in the next room and that I must keep standing up like this in one place or another and clutch onto tangible realities to be faced—me and the sheet of glass—and the unrelenting feel of it against my palms and not expect or hope for anything more ever except the capacity to recognise reality. Reality had become me on one side of the glass and a foggy London night on the other; street lights outside and cars driving by and the necessity only of deciding what minute details of living to perform next.

They wouldn't let me go in to him. It had happened as I was coming up in the lift and when the lift stopped at his floor nurses and doctors were hurrying down the passage to his room. I sent messages: I asked the house doctor to tell him I was there outside but there was no time for messages, or place, or room around that crowded bed where they worked to restore rhythm to his heart. I don't know what he felt, or thought, or said—if he asked for me, or was frightened, or just again possessed by pain. I only know now that I should have forced my way in. It would have made no difference to his death, but perhaps to his dying. He did it alone, under the anaesthetic when they opened up his chest once more to massage that valiant heart. And I sat, surrounded this time, four hours later, by his family whom I had telephoned, but also alone, and felt him die without me. I knew it—the moment of his death. A cold and shocking shiver took hold of me: blankets were brought and brandy, but nothing took away the cold, and that, I am certain, was the moment of his dying. An hour later they came in and told me, and life without him began.

CHAPTER 16

MAGGY CAME and slept in the house that night. She read Lisa her bedtime story, telephoned the rest of Emmet's family, placed an announcement in the *Times*, and tucked me into bed with a hotwater bottle and sedatives.

My brother-in-law came the next morning to drive me to the hospital. I signed a piece of paper giving permission for an autopsy. The doctor told me it would help others. I held my hand over the words so that I could not read what I was signing. Driving through Hyde Park on the way to the hospital and back, the trees and the traffic signals, the dogs and their owners, the passing cars, the clouds in the sky, all seemed etched in bold outline, strong colours, larger and closer than remembered. I was seeing them for the first time as if through eyes peeled of a skin, gingerly, feeling my body wrapped in a protective but nevertheless fragile film. On the borderline of, but more intense than, consciousness. This sensation lasted for some days—days in which exterior life went on around me and a part of me entered into it but only a part. I was drugged each night into sleep; the worst time was first awakening—the feeling of unnamed dread before eyes open—not fully conscious enough to identify the dread but clutched in its embrace.

For some days after Emmet's death, copious and carefully chosen hampers were delivered from Johnny Hannay at the Savoy: delicious custards, pureed vegetables, cakes and ice creams and fruit for the children; heartening soups and casseroles for the adults—champagne, foie gras and caviar to cheer away the evening tear. The hampers were collected the following day with strict instructions not to bother washing the dishes. Anonymous expressions of care and compassion were the most moving. I resolved to learn from this experience how heart-warming these can be. A beautiful coat for Lisa, claiming eternal love from the White House, a small fortune in couture for a three-year-old; on Christmas Eve a fat envelope stuffed full of £5 notes pushed through my letterbox—with no hint ever of the donors.

Sadly my grandmother's largesse was not to have a happy ending for me. Two weeks before she died, bedridden and alone except for a coterie of elderly harpies—now claiming lifelong friendship, with their sights set on what remained of the cut glass and the silver menu holders—and prone to the influence of her remaining sisters, she changed her will. Presumably, secure in the belief that a liquid fortune gurgled happily away in some subterranean treasure chest she divided her estate, hitherto totally mine, into two—three quarters to me and the remaining quarter to a variety of bizarre charities. One week later she added a codicil, reducing my three quarters by a series of bequests to individuals, not least to her aged doctor who was therefore disinclined to assist in a query of her mental stability. I would not ever suspect my splendid grandmother of becoming senile, even at ninety-four, but I expect her standards remained those of the champagne in the cellar. The charities chosen were bizarre only inasmuch as they had touched little on her life, apart from substantial poetry grants to every school and University college attended by my uncle, and I wonder which of the harpies steered her to the eminently worthy Royal Lifesaving Society, or the Home for Spastic Children? Silver, china, lace, all trappings of my memory of life with her, and photographs, simply disappeared. There was, of course, no cash. The house remained—a potential goldmine, but now divided into quarters and so forced into a sale; and into the hands of the long-suffering but now powerful estate agents who had been her tenants. My father refused in the face of death to have anything more to do with her than he had in life, and so, distant as I was, both geographically in England and emotionally as a young mother, I left the will in the hands of her new executors and became, overnight, a poor relation. I had not been brought up to play the part. Only years later did I bother to reflect on my lost inheritance when I heard that the site of the house was no longer a Sex Arcade but the main Kings Cross Underground Station and at last reckoning had changed hands at very many millions. Now, for the first time, I felt the loss of them.

But, if my children lacked the Nana and Great Aunt Juliet of my youth, they had a fairy godmother and godfather. The night Emmet died I sent a telegram to Chula and Lisba, on their annual trip to Thailand. The answering cable, from Lisba, assumed the responsibility for Lisa's education from that day through university. I also telephoned our dear friend Steven Runciman on his island, Eigg, off the coast of Scotland. Steven caught the sleeper to London, and the next night over dinner at my kitchen table, told me that he wished to similarly educate his goddaughter, Lisa.

'Oh, Steven,' I said, 'How wonderful of you but Lisba has just offered.'

'Very well then—I'll take the boy.'

How incredibly blessed I was with such friends.

* * *

I was prepared for trials and hardship and misery and the long drawn-out business of living for the children. It was a dramatic picture—visions of unlikely occupations filled my pondering hours. I saw myself in a flower shop, or as someone's house-keeper. The someone had no face but the flowers did and I have never been particularly good with flowers. People talked to me of courage and how one could possibly manage alone; of how we would survive, of the healing of time.

This last seemed to me an insult; I did not wish to be healed of my memories. Time, in any event, does not heal: it overtakes. You can't worry about bringing up children when they're growing up from under you. You can't pull in on the hard shoulder and watch the traffic go by. You can't worry about the overall business of being lonely when each fresh disaster has to be met head on. Children's routines carried me along.

When Emmet died, England was water-logged, grey, cold, and terrifying. I had bad bronchitis for the first and only time in my life—evidence of the link between mind, heart and body. I had little ready money and a large, expensive house which was suddenly transformed into a hungry monster, eating it up. Emmet's father and friends all urged me to move house. Bad advice, I would now tell the bereaved. Happy memories inhabit happy walls. I wish I had always stayed in the house in which we had lived: I wish I lived in it now. I wish I had not rushed to give away all Emmet's clothes. He is always in my mind, just behind the seeing eye, but how I wish there was a familiar room, a familiar chair, in which I could place him. We should not try to run away from pain: it has its place, sometimes a sweet place.

Sometimes, since, in bad times, that pain has given me strength: a sense of proportion. Then, I have wanted only to remember the blood—thick and smooth and red, red, red—as he spat it out. I have wanted to remember the hard things—I have wanted to be back there where I was living, living as he was dying and we were together. I have been part of him again, hugging his back in the dark, with him as we turned on the light so he could see where to spit the blood. No conflict, no decisions to be taken alone, the smooth feel of his strong, strong shoulders as I hugged them in the dark. He spat out the blood in the baby's blue pot. It had a yellow duck for him to cling to as he sat. When the blood came too thick and fast for the pot we measured it in his feeding bottle, and I emptied each full bottle down the lavatory after recording it for the doctor, so we knew each day how much he had lost.

Only blood he lost—not heart, or strength, or love, or humour. In the times between the pain and the coughing we slept rolled up together like two nuts, two peas, two birds entwined; I around him, holding on to his warmth and strength—not sapped by loss of blood, only touched by a tiny chill of fear, too weak to shake us in our cocoon.

It still envelops me—the cocoon—and, when needed, Emmet reaches out his hand to me.

CHAPTER 17

HAVING BEEN brought up, happily, by my mother and grandmother to despise money, it remained, and still lingers on in my
mind, a dirty word. My grandmother, if forced to mention it,
would call it 'filthy lucre', where in the back of my mind it remains
in a rosy cloud of indifference. A lot of it came from mysterious
people called the Perpetual Trustees who were connected with
rich, dead Great Uncle Harry, and through him to his widow,
rich, foolish, generous Great Aunt Juliet. How Uncle Harry had
obtained this money was never disclosed in my childhood. Aunt
Juliet called it 'dear, darling Harry' as she telephoned the face-
less trustees, her only remaining link with Uncle Harry. I knew

that Daddy worked very hard as a doctor; I knew that there were many people who never paid him money, nor did he send them bills. Bills were things which came through the post and were addressed to Mummy, hurriedly glanced at before being stuffed into a kitchen drawer and sometimes taken out and given to the Perpetual Trustees when Aunt Juliet felt generous. Many school friends had many sheep and many cows and bullocks in thousands of sun-baked acres in what we called 'the bush'. I did not wonder if these cost money or earned money: they were their equivalent of the kitchen drawer.

I am somewhat grateful for this training. It engenders a sense of unassailable security. If money is never real, its loss is a chimera.

I very much wish, of course, that I had not rushed to sell anything that I thought could raise money: my problem being the paucity of immediate cash. I am sick to think of what I then recklessly sold, often to any crook who came to the door. Family silver had long since gone, but there was a fine hoard of wedding present substitutes, and jewellery. A Georgian silver sugar coaster, a gift from film star Alan Ladd, went for a few pounds. I had lost so much weight that clothes went, too—all the remaining Dior New Looks. I thought of our cellar, bursting with wine and of the dinner parties I would never give again.

One of the more immediate and seductive delights of my Thai job had been the opportunity to acquire, at duty-free prices, an impressive cellar. I had long dabbled in a love of wine, unsupported by much knowledge although I liked to consider myself an expert, and boasted untruthfully of being a member of the august body of Tastevins. My bogus claim to this was not entirely without truthful foundation, but owed something to an alcoholic mist over the memory of my so-called training. On a trip through France sometime in the 1950s, Stanley Haynes and I had dallied in a village in the middle of the vineyards of Châteauneuf-du-Pape. We visited, as are all tourists encouraged to do, the local cellars, somehow made friends with 'le Patron' and stayed a month, during which time I, euphemistically, helped. I remember hot, happy, damp and smelly afternoons spitting and swallowing, and tramping about in a haze of enthusiasm and alcohol. I did learn something, albeit from the aegis of a not particularly distinguished grape, and I remember that on taking our fond farewells some sort of embossed scroll was pressed into my hands. This, although long since lost, became, in my mind, my privileged entrée into the world of wine connoisseurs.

It did, nevertheless, stand me in good stead. I started to buy wine books and learn more. I realised how fortunate I had been in having a few startlingly clear early memories of imbibing. My grandmother's oft-proffered glass of champagne had always been a good vintage from a grande marque. My first known experience of a great wine had also stuck in my mind because of its incongruous association. When I was seventeen or so, at a barbecue lunch at Palm Beach near Sydney—hot and sticky in swimsuits, gathered round the sausages—dear rich and generous Arthur Browning had insisted on pouring a bottle of Château d'Yquem into a bowl of particularly nasty tinned cream of chicken soup. He explained that this was how soup was served in Europe. Having no knowledge of that great glamorous distant world, I decided that when and if I got there, I would steer clear of soup.

The next time I encountered Château d'Yquem was my first country weekend in England at luncheon with David's mother. With our pudding (at least I had learned between the ages of seventeen and twenty-four that it did not go into the soup) she gave us a bottle remaining from the cellars of Imperial Russia. It was a rich, deep, golden brown: I can't remember the year but as her father, the Grand Duke Michael, had spirited it out of Russia with him before the Revolution in 1917, I imagine it may have been the late 1890s, and the date does ring some sort of a tinkle. But I do remember the taste, and the perfume. I understood for the first time the use of the word 'nectar'. So Château d'Yquem became for me a landmark in my lexicon of wines.

The second fortuitous circumstance was the fact that my husband drank hardly at all, and smoked seldom. He had had to give up the smoking early in our acquaintance on discovering his heart condition, and had begun, with me, to drink wine for the first time in his life. As soon as my appointment to the Thai Embassy in London became official I sent off for all the wine catalogues from the leading wine merchants and began to realise how cheaply I could stock what was, miraculously, a proper London wine cellar. There can be few left, but ours was stone built, stone rack upon rack in arched soaring ranks, with a solid thick door, and approached through a small courtyard rather than down a flight of rickety stairs. It was dry, cool and commodious and had been built for no other purpose.

The third astonishing happening was that it was quickly discovered that Emmet had what I was assured by some of our new wine-merchant friends that rarity, a perfect palate. As the crates of wine were delivered Emmet read all my wine books. Soon he could be blindfolded and identify immediately the wine, and often the vintage. He was invited by Berry Bros, Saccone & Speed and the like to luncheons in the city where he became a prize exhibit. I never equalled it: mine was book knowledge, and now I have even forgotten that. What is left is our first cellar book, and sad reading it makes. Bottle after priceless bottle of glorious liquid was squandered nightly on whomever happened to come to dine—few of them appreciative, I fear.

The cellar book, started in 1953, reads:

Ch. Margaux, 1953, ch.b. 22/6p.

Ch. Mouton Rothschild, 1952, ch.b. 25/-.

Ch. Mouton Rothschild, 1947, ch.b.

Ch. Margaux, 1945, 30/-.

Ch. Lafite, 1947, 1 magnum—no price listed.

Ch. Lafite, 1953, 22/-6p.

Ch. Latour, 1953, 22/-6p.

Ch. Calon-Ségur, 1937, 26/-6p.

Ch. Haut-Brion, 1947, 21/-6p.

Ch. Haut-Brion, 1953, 22/-6p.

Ch. Cheval Blanc, 1952, 22/-6p.

Vosne-Romanée, 1947, no price listed.

Richebourg, 1947, 19/-6p.

...and so on to lesser growths, like Léoville-Barton, Lynch-Bages, Palmer, Léoville-Las Cases, dismissed in the shilling class. The great whites, the Puligny Montrachets, and the Meursault Charmes, are not dignified by price either.

Remorse prevents me from contemplating the guests, most of them quite unaware of what they were drinking. I am proud, however, of the food. I was learning to be a good cook. Removed from the telephone instructions of my mother's cook, I turned, as did most of England's postwar generation, to Elizabeth David.

As I moved house after Emmet's death, so the cellar—then and in subsequent moves—became a major problem; second only, if not equal, to what to do with the books.

But at the time the wine could be said to be a financial asset as well as a storage liability. I had never met the wine writer Cyril Ray, but he had heard of my hoard and wrote to me. After some polite sentences of commiseration on the death of my husband he came quickly to the point.

He had heard I had one of the finest small private cellars in England. Would I consider selling part, if not all, of it?

Lists of available wines went between us. He would take all, of course, but marked his preferences, accompanied by expressions of anticipated joy in the drinking, if I wished to retain some. The final list was drawn up, price agreed, and Cyril Ray, no doubt, had planned his first dinner party.

I had two brooches left—both should have had the sentimental value I now, too late, bestow on them. One, all diamonds, was my mother's; the other, diamond and emerald, a present from David—both still in their Cartier boxes. I sold them at Sotheby's and kept the wine, explaining the switch to Cyril Ray, who wrote me a letter of congratulations.

'Despite my own disappointment, I salute the most civilised act I have ever seen performed by a woman.'

Sometimes now, along with contemplation of those unworthy gullets down which disappeared most of my wine, I see similar brooches to mine displayed in auction-room catalogues, estimates well into the double if not triple thousands. I received £30 each from the Sotheby's sale.

Not all the wine was drunk in the immediate years after Emmet's death. Some twelve years later, settled in a larger and grander, but cellarless, house, I kept a stock of everyday 'drinking' wines in the proverbial cupboard (although a basement cupboard) under the stairs and the dwindling stock of first-growth clarets in a wholly unsuitable walk-in cupboard in one of the unused attic rooms. There were some of the 45s, most of the 61s, and four precious bottles of d'Yquem 37. We had an Irish couple of some incompetence, as cook/general and gardener/*homme à tout faire*, but of seeming honesty and undoubted good humour. The Spanish daily had just left and a new one engaged as we set off on holiday. A month later we came home, to find a clean house, but were greeted by Mr O'Leary with the news that they didn't hold much store by this new one, yet another Maria, as she spent most of her time gossiping at the kitchen table from which vantage point she had frequently offered them a glass of wine.

'Mrs O'Leary and I, we never touch the stuff,' he stoutly professed.

What stuff, I wondered idly. The wine cupboard did not seem depleted to me. Mr O'Leary simply sniffed when interrogated further. It wasn't until the next day that I thought of the attic cupboard, soon found empty. Sixty-six irreplaceable bottles had gone. It was a Friday: Maria would not appear again until the Monday morning, but the first people I thought of were my insurance company.

They immediately notified the police. It was out of my hands, and reluctantly and feeling both foolish and unkind I gave them Maria's address, the O'Learys having repeated their saga of the kitchen table orgies.

Maria and her husband were flabbergasted. All those old bottles had been covered in dust and cobwebs—obviously forgotten and of no value to anyone. No wine could possibly cost more than 50p per bottle when new and presentable. There was nothing left to salvage, except a stack of empty bottles outside their door.

To their eternal credit, the insurance company paid up, the first time in their history they had had such a claim. We settled eventually on the sum of an average of £11 per bottle. I suppose in the 1970s this was a fair price. Similar bottles now fetch thousands in auctions but I daresay I would have found yet more unworthy but eager gullets by now and should instead count myself lucky to have had the £700. I would rather have the diamond brooches.

But I have skimmed forward in time. Back in 1957, I began to regret the splendid hedonistic disregard for worldly goods with which I had been brought up, the lavish life style of my mother and grandmother and great aunt which in following had managed to leave me stranded on an uncomfortably barren ledge.

CHAPTER 18

ONE DAY came a letter from an acquaintance, a girl whom I had met once at a luncheon party, suggesting that I go and share her life in Italy. She was Swedish, divorced from a Russian: her baby son the same age as mine, and I had, from the chance luncheon encounter, inherited her Italian nanny.

'Come here,' she wrote. 'I am living in the most beautiful place imaginable, in a cottage in a heavenly park. Wild doves, peacocks, dogs, cats, chickens and horses everywhere—yesterday a horse walked into the dining room. The Contessa, whose estate this is, would let me a 15th Century Tower, part of the main villa, for almost nothing: but it is too big for me. We could divide it in two, and we could share Brunella (our nanny)...' I don't know why I should have assumed, for the first time in my life, that it was desirable to have a horse in one's dining room, but I was carried away by her enthusiasm, by the vision she painted of sunshine, Italy and escape—and by the sudden idea of letting my demanding London house.

There were many more letters, always with the pattern of peacocks, peace, doves and solitude uppermost, but also necessary mentions of more realistic living arrangements. I was to have the upper two floors of the tower, consisting of two bedrooms and a bathroom for myself, children and Brunella, and the attic where the doves lived. She was to sleep with her small son in one bedroom, with bath, on the ground floor adjoining our communal living room and kitchen. Somewhere among the increasingly jubilant flow of letters I discovered that my part of the tower was accessible only by an outside spiral staircase. Conditioned by nursery gates, barred windows and Pye talk boxes, I protested that I could not thus be cut off from the children after their bedtime.

'Don't worry,' she carolled back. 'All will work out—we will change if you wish. Anyway, there are many possibilities.' Quite obviously, from her first rough sketch of the tower, there were not; but with far more innocence and far less suspicion than I was later to view the relatively urban dwellings offered me by villa-renting establishments, I accepted her words, and, at last, we left.

The tower was in a tiny village, Fino Mornasco, above Lake Como. I had not driven our car much during four and a half years of marriage and two pregnancies, but as it seemed essential for our future life, I decided to drive, via the Dover–Boulogne car ferry. Only Brunella viewed the venture darkly. She didn't really want to go back to Italy, and, most of all, she wanted nothing to do with her former employer. 'You will see, Signora,' she wailed. 'The Principessa'—for such she was—'is mad!'

I bought a splendid collapsible drop-sided cot from Harrods, which was to serve Seamus as a bed in car, ship, train and tower. Wedged inside it in the back of the car, he looked like some cherubic inhabitant of a human zoo, and he played and slept happily right across Europe. Nappy changing was a bore, and often back-breaking, trying not to dislodge the cot whilst dislodging the nappies. Putting the cot up in our three-berth sleeper meant that there was not an inch of space for undressing or even standing, so that Brunella, Lisa and I had to leap from door straight into bunk and wriggle out of our clothes once there. The channel crossing was the roughest I have ever experienced. After one look at the choppy sea I had grabbed the last available private cabin, and so we were all four able to be sick in comparative luxury. A helpful young cabin boy walked up and down holding Seamus, who vomited periodically down his back. Brunella grabbed our bathroom before we left port and spent the crossing groaning and effectively blocking the lavatory with her head. I lay on one bunk being sick and trying to comfort my daughter who lay on the other, whimpering. By the time we reached France, the cabin boy had whisked down below, changed his clothing, and washed and dried Seamus's.

Just before we arrived at Dover, Lisa had said: 'Mummy, what's that on Seamus's finger?'

'Where?' Half-looking, too busy to show much interest, desperate to get to the ferry and out of the country, and with no time for trivialities, I glimpsed, nonetheless, out of the corner of my eye, a shiny, angry, puce lump with a bright yellow centre engaging one third of the total circumference of Seamus's middle finger. It did not appear to be a triviality. In Dover, I had had time to telephone my doctor in London and visit the local hospital. The hospital doctor had bandaged it, told me to put hot poultices on it all night, and to go to a doctor the moment we reached Lyon. 'If you notice red streaks travelling up his arm,' he said casually, 'that's the danger sign.' My own doctor thought perhaps I'd better start giving him oral penicillin right away. Being a doctor's daughter and widow, I was full of half knowledge, antibiotic prejudices and terror: so I decided against the penicillin, only to find there was no hot water on the train.

By Lyon, his tiny finger was all swelling—now with a greenish black centre—no red streaks. Lisa had been sick in her bunk in the night and had spent the remainder in mine. There was no restaurant car on the train. We tottered to a large hotel in Lyon, ordered breakfast, washed and demanded a doctor. The concierge directed me instead to the hospital, as I told him I was in a hurry to leave town. Sitting over breakfast coffee, I thought for the only time in my life that I was going to faint—fatigue, worry and travel nausea hit me with a wave, and if there had been a man anywhere in the world to whom I could have sent

162

a plea, 'Come and get me', we would never have reached our tower. Instead we went to the hospital, where we were shunted into Casualty. There, I spent four hours of horror. The doctors and their assistants were brutal, dirty and blood spattered. Cigarettes hung from the corners of their mouths and my tiny son was strapped, under a powerful light, to an operating table for nearly an hour before they operated, without anaesthetic, on his finger. It took four men to hold him down. I think local application of heat and a needle prick might have sufficed, but I was too cowed by terror of those red streaks to protest.

Perhaps by contrast, the remainder of our drive to the Italian border was calm and pleasant. The children fitted in with any timetable of eating or sleeping which suited us. As Brunella spoke no French, and was an island girl from Capri with no previous travel experience beyond her original trip to England with the Principessa, I was virtually in charge of three children; but I treasured the thought that once across the Italian border I could relax and leave much of the necessary arrangements to Brunella.

I was soon to discover that I could not rely on Brunella's Italian either: she spoke the Caprese dialect, and glared with resentment at the northerners who attempted to communicate with her.

We arrived in Milano in driving rain. Cots, pots, playpens and prams were tethered to the roof of our car by the most feminine of knots and I had omitted to cover anything with a tarpaulin; so most of our belongings were both precariously perched and drenched. Cars shot at us, horns blaring and tyres screeching, from out of torrents of rain, and I screamed at passers-by in pidgin Italian for directions. Brunella was determined on only one thing—that we must stop and buy the bare necessities for the children's evening meal before we left Milano. I thought it eccentric of her to imagine that my co-tenant would not be waiting with a warm and well-stocked welcome, but to keep her happy I agreed. She scooted off through the rain and came back armed with packages, reiterating, 'You don't know the Principessa.'

Fino Mornasco proved to be a half-hour drive from Milano. The rain had settled into a steady downpour when we arrived at the huge iron gates of the villa. The drive and the vast villa looked deserted and forbidding in the gathering darkness. Great trees banged against the windows of the car and wet leaves swept across the windscreen. There was no sign of dove, peacock, horse, or human. The children started to cry. The tower came into sight as we rounded the drive—romantic and beautiful, perhaps—but dark, dank and deserted certainly, and covered in copiously dripping creepers. Banging on doors finally produced a helpful house guest of the Contessa's, who in turn produced a toothless hag with a key—large, rusty and ancient. We drove on down the drive under an arch of dripping magnolias, and let ourselves into the tower.

There was a letter from the Principessa to say she was spending the night in Milano—she hoped I would be comfortable. There was no fire, no hot water, no food of any kind. Brunella was right—the Principessa was not to be relied upon...

CHAPTER 19

THE TOWER wasn't a tower in the sense of it being part of another, larger, structure. It was simply one room on top of another—three in all—becoming increasingly narrower as it rose. We all managed to live, eat and cook on the ground floor in a large salon and antiquated kitchen, and the Principessa and son slept in the adjoining room. As she had warned me, my room shared with the children was above this, as was my tiny bathroom, finished all but for a gaping hole in the wall at the end of the bath. Through this hole an endless procession of lizards and spiders crawled to watch me bathe. Perched on top, yet again, was Brunella's room. The staircase was narrow and slippery—disastrously so in the rain—and wound precariously round the outside of the building.

A woman friend, Sheila Smart, came out from England to keep me company and was accommodated in a cottage in the stable block amongst the pregnant dogs, hens, pigs and peasant retainers. She was my only ally against the charming but totally unscrupulous Principessa, and we took it in turns to cook the meals and release the field mice each morning from the Italian traps set for them by the Principessa the previous night. The mouse traps were square houses, not so small as not to be palatial to a field mouse, well stocked with cheese; and the grateful mice we set free on the tennis court each morning must have broadcast its comforts, and limited dangers, as the traps became ever more populous.

The cooking was a more hazardous affair. Whoever touched the oven door received a fairly hefty electric shock. We boiled or fried our food as much as possible.

The children thrived. Brunella was my rock. I did not miss my husband in the sense that I missed him later, and in cities. It was a time of peace and adjustment, embalmed in boredom and country events, enlivened only by the necessity to make minor decisions. Our days were spent lying in the spring and early summer sunshine by the concrete swimming pool. The pool had been a handsome legacy left by the occupying Germans who had commandeered the villa during the war. Alas, the Contessa could not swim and though happy for our sakes to have the pool, was determined that it should cause her no personal discomfort.

Each day she would arrive in our midst in a splendidly frilled romper suit with parasol to match, with her shining black plaits of hair wound round her ears, followed by Michaele. Michaele was neither butler, nor gardener, nor bailiff, but something of all three, his duties ranging from mending a fuse to killing the poisonous frogs—deadly I was told—who frolicked in the pool and on our bathroom window sills each morning. When the Contessa arrived we would exchange our morning pleasantries while Michaele killed the frogs and occasionally a snake.

Then, her parasol aloft to protect the gleaming black dye on her hair from the sun, she would wade into the two feet of water which were our daily ration and lie on the bottom—feet and bloomer frills floating gently on the surface. In these two murky feet my children gradually learned to swim: we adults could do no more than duck. Seamus began to talk—a hideous Caprese dialect being his first language—and my friend Sheila and I devised our rigid social life.

At 4 o'clock each day the train to Milano passed through the village station and in the station waiting room were sold the best ice creams in all Italy, and, so it follows, in all the world. At 3 o'clock Sheila and I dressed ourselves carefully, made up our faces and did our hair, and walked the mile or so to the station to watch the 4 o'clock train go by, eating our ice cream of the day. The flavours were raspberry, strawberry, nougat, pistachio, lemon, peppermint, vanilla—the daily decision an agony. A few workmen played dominoes at one of the other tables: we exchanged daily nods.

Occasionally, we actually caught the 4 o'clock train to Milano and spent an evening at La Scala. Once we were late: the train was pulling out of the station as we came round the top of the hill and started to run, hampered horribly by our wooden clogs (a hangover from rationed shoes). The guard saw us, pulled out his whistle; the driver stopped the train and all the male passengers clapped and shouted in unison as we clattered down the hill—'Due bella signora!' Due bella signora!'—and then hauled us aboard.

Sometimes we went back to the villa and dressed up once more to drink an after-dinner coffee with the Contessa and her house guests. They were all of them old generals, mouldering Russian princesses, Austrian barons escaping from a more vague boredom to our life of tiny and precise discipline. That is what it was—the discipline of doing nothing and yet occupying the mind and senses—a discipline since forgotten, its loss sadly regretted. We were given one tiny, strong black cup of coffee each and one tiny, strong glass of Strega; and we sat gossiping under the light of the twenty-five-watt chandelier in the gilded and brocaded splendour of the palazzo, peering at each other through the gloom. Sheila and I bought stronger light bulbs for our own quarters but lived in fear of being caught using too much electricity, it being included in the rent. We also devised a much more satisfying drink for the nights we were not invited to join the Contessa. A bottle of the cheapest grappa poured in the morning into two glasses of raisins would swell by evening into a drink of rich and fiery delight.

As we settled in to this routine I had no plans for the future. The house in London was let for two years—perhaps at some later date we would visit my father in Australia—and meanwhile there was wonderful, sturdy, cheerful, constant Brunella for me to lean on. One day Brunella seemed less cheerful; the next she sang not at all; on the third she said she did not feel well, and thought she should see a doctor. The local doctor had already been encountered over the affair of Seamus's finger, and so I took Brunella to see him.

She emerged smiling. 'Is not serious,' she explained. 'Is making tests. For getting in Como in three days.' She sang again. I gave her not another thought beyond wondering how I could ever manage without her in my life again.

In three days, I was driving into Como and Brunella asked me if I would pick up the results of her tests. Still naively unsuspecting, I paid over the counter what seemed a disproportionately large sum of money—for what? For a slip of paper on which was written one word: 'POSITIVO'.

I spoke hardly any Italian: it was not necessary. All was clear. 'Brunella,' I said, 'Is it possible you are going to have a baby?' ('Oh, God,' I thought, 'not another baby!') Brunella burst into tears: in between wailing about her mother in Capri she assured me it was not possible because she was virgin but that Forte was a very naughty man. Forte, she enlightened me, was her fiancé—very rich, very Greek, very naughty. Forte had made her do something on our last night in London, but she did not know what: she was virgin and so she did not understand.

Dimly, I remembered our last hectic night—scuffles on the stairs late at night, a dark, polite face encountered at the door on other nights asking for Brunella. Now, having divested herself of her problem to me, it became my problem—Mama in Capri, the baby, Forte. All was up to me, with Brunella eagerly complying with all suggestions. The secure thought of Brunella in my life forever vanished: I would be left alone in what had suddenly become an abyss of the unknown and Brunella must be packed off to London and to her hitherto unsuspected and unsuspecting fiancé. First, the fiancé must be informed and Brunella had every intention that I should tell him. They had little language in common and none that both of them could write. Thus began the long history of my correspondence with Brunella's lovers; imperceptibly, I had gained a third child.

Forte, as a lover, was quickly disposed of. To my calm and indulgent letter, assuring him of my care for Brunella and asking only for details of her return journey, he replied 'Dear Dalton—I know not of what you speak.' Further letters ended in abrupt and angry silence. Brunella wept a great deal and wailed louder about Mama and how she would kill her. I foresaw once again the permanence of Brunella in my life, but with an added problem—her baby.

But she was determined not to have the baby, and in this I could not shake her. My Italian was barely a month old, not equal to the task of finding an obliging doctor in Milano. The local doctor was out of the question. I hung around the likeliest of the Austrian baronesses one night after coffee, and in the smoothest conversational tone I could muster, asked her if she knew of a good abortionist nearby.

She was a duck, that baroness. Hers is a name I shall never forget—Litzi Thun. A council of war was held next day over morning coffee in her room and distant acquaintances were dug up—each one further removed from Brunella. Names were provided who could supply other names and we had now only to do battle with the telephone.

I had no telephone. I had a contraption on the wall of the salon, in full range of the beady eye and eager ear of the Principessa, which was a sort of one-way extension from the main telephone in the palazzo. The one way was a capricious arrangement— sometimes I could hear the other party—sometimes they could hear me. About half the time some somnolent servant lurking in the dim corners of the main house actually answered the tinkle and connected me to the outside world. From then on, it was anyone's guess as to who was hearing whom. But a doctor was indeed located in Milano, and, in a series of frustrating calls, it was established that he would see Brunella, would perform the operation, would keep her in his clinic overnight, and would charge eighty guineas.

I could not leave the children. Sheila was delegated to take Brunella and it was agreed that they should go separately and meet on the steps of the Duomo in time to go together to the doctor. The day was baking hot. Sheila left early for a day's sightseeing in Milano and I put Brunella on our 4 o'clock train. Sheila was a handsome and elegant woman, sympathetic and capable and not apt to be unduly disturbed by the ambience, whatever it should prove to be, of an abortionist's rooms, being of an age best described as 'past child-bearing'. However, the day having been exceedingly hot and tiring, she was in some despair when Brunella had not appeared well past the appointed time when they could still have met the appointment. Best to go to the doctor on her own and explain she had lost Brunella. The doctor was in an apartment building a bus ride away. A considerably more hot, tired and dusty Sheila found the door only some ten minutes late and pressed the bell. In no time, she was let in, pounced on, surrounded, and nearly strapped down before she was able to convince the eager and aggressive nurse that it was not nerves which made her reluctant to undress and submit, but mistaken identity. But, contact was made, and so was another appointment. Brunella was found, at the wrong end of Milano, and she lost her baby on another appointed day.

The summer drifted by. The Principessa left in a flurry of unpaid bills; the Contessa and I became fused in friendship by our joint ill-treatment at her hands. Our involvement in the life of the villa was enlarged to include invitations to watch excruciating television programmes—all chosen by the Contessa's husband who, inexplicably, was never addressed as 'Count', but always, by all including his wife, as 'Enginere'. The Contessa had seemingly married beneath her in the social sphere but not in matters of influence. The tubby little *enginere* had built some of the grander of Mussolini's roads and buildings and, having been suitably financially rewarded in Il Duce's day and created his Finance Minister, was never thereafter allowed to forget it. If he fitted at all into a scheme of life at the villa, it was as an engineer and, for want of a more appropriate title, that is what he would be called.

Sometimes we went on picnics on the lake—to an island where we were rowed in a flotilla of little boats by footmen who then laid out white damask, wine buckets, delicious food, and waited on us at the water's edge. Michaele came along to hold the parasol over the Contessa's head as she billowed in the water. No picnic has seemed worthy of the name since, no water more limpid or dappled with sunlight, no feast more luxurious, or wine more tantalising, no setting more idyllic.

In September, the fogs began swirling up and around the shores of the lake and down from the Alps, blanketing our little community in damp greyness. The generals and the barons began their farewells; relatives were remembered in cosier climates, and it became evident that we, too, must move on.

Other arrivals during that year, at other houses, as we moved slowly down Italy following the sun, were fraught with shock and despair, but none had been so complete as our first cold, damp night in our tower. But somehow, I look back upon our months at Fino Mornasco as calm, peaceful and regulated. I, too, remember the doves and the peacocks pecking food from our table, the beauty of the park, the sunshine, and the delightful Contessa. I have forgotten the agony of worry caused by the tiny outside stone staircase and the sheer drop from the tower windows; the field mice in our beds and cots; the capricious water supply; the lethal stove; the mad Principessa. As we left Milano, I felt great sadness. Brunella looked back along the autostrada—'Mama Mia, Mrs Dalton. I leave plenty memory behind me here,' she said mournfully.

* * *

We took a hideous modern apartment next, at Sori, near Genoa. The view was breathtaking and made up for the veneer of our dining-room sideboard, the Burmese gongs and three-piece suite. It was built on a bend of the coast, perched above the main coastal road and nothing was to be seen from the windows but the sparkling sea and rocky cliffs. Peace was visual—not aural. Lambrettas and Lamborghinis shrieked round the bend below our windows night and day. Slower and more commodious vehicles had their radios on full blast. They hooted at each other incessantly. The children and Brunella slept at the front of the apartment directly above this parade; my bedroom was at the back in relative quiet. Until the night I was shaken awake by Brunella wailing, 'Mama Mia—come quick—house falling down—get children quick!' It did not seem to me inconceivable that we could in fact topple off our bit of cliff onto the road below, and so I sprang from bed expecting the ground to tremble beneath me. 'Where, Brunella? How?' I entreated as the ground remained remarkably firm. 'Big noise,' she cried, 'Awful noise. Me fright.' There had indeed been a most appalling crash directly beneath her window: a huge lorry hung, headlights streaking far out to sea, half off the road edge—another crumpled van across the road; but to look out the window had been for Brunella far too fearsome a thing—far better to get me and retreat up the mountain side at our backs as best we could.

As the children had to be propelled across this road if we wanted to reach the village or the beach far below us it was clear that Sori must be only a temporary stop. It served to advance the children's swimming, begun in the concrete pool and now aided by rubber alligators in the Mediterranean. Seamus had his second birthday in a rowing boat, captained by a beautiful and insistent young Italian whom I had picked up, hopefully for Brunella, but whose object soon turned out to be to get me to the local dance hall. '*Per che non ballare?*' he repeated plaintively day after day as he rowed me and the children out to sea and Brunella giggled on the shore.

The sun was retreating southwards—Brunella had not seen her family for more than a year—Capri was, to me, a picture postcard name, a place for youthful visits never taken but not a haven—but I agreed to go as far south as Positano and at least look at Capri. And so, granny knots tethering our belongings to roof racks once more, we went off.

I installed us in a grand hotel in Salerno where, in nearby Positano, I had a painter friend, Peter Ruta. The children went to bed: Brunella and I shared a splendid room-service dinner at the foot of Seamus's cot. She was ecstatic. She had come home in great style.

The next day, Peter, Brunella, the children and I set off on a day trip to Capri. By the end of that day I had rented a four-bed-room house looking out towards via Tragara and the Faraglioni and had returned to Salerno for our belongings. I left the car in a garage on the mainland and sent for a friend of Emmet's to come out and stay with us, drive the car home, and sell it—the equivalent of boat burning.

* * *

Capri was an instant seduction. I have never seen it in summer, but in autumn, winter and spring, it beguiled and charmed. Brunella had eleven brothers and sisters, a mother, father and various nieces and nephews on the island. I wanted for nothing: a sister sewed for me; a nephew delivered the vegetables; a brother kept my evening table at a cafe in the square. The children made friends with the younger nephews and nieces—I made friends with a few charming residents—friends came out from England to stay—and here, I thought, I shall settle. The children will go to the local school and will grow up Italian.

I began to sense a permanence and stability in our lives. There was a village school; there were new friends; there was Brunella. Perhaps the time had come to get Seamus christened as a good Italian Catholic. Emmet and I had never had the time between illnesses. And so Brunella was dispatched to the local priest, an appointment made, all of us interviewed, and a date and local godparents set.

Nearer the day, when a cake had been ordered and his putative godfather, a delightful Italian nobleman, 'Franchi' Lanfranchi, had organised the christening party, we had word from the priest cancelling the ceremony. It seemed that the Bishop of Naples, whose diocese we were in, refused to sanction it because I was neither a Catholic nor a guaranteed permanent resident.

Dr Cuomo was the only doctor on the island; so when Seamus developed a large lump in his neck gland and a daily fever we all bundled off through the ferocious winter storms to Dr Cuomo. From Dr Cuomo we were sent to Naples on the churning winter sea to the International Hospital, for X-rays. There were four trips across the bay, numerous trips to Dr Cuomo, when finally tuberculosis was diagnosed, and Seamus was injected with a fearsome dose of antibiotics. Dr Cuomo was far too grand to visit himself; so a fat and dirty woman appeared twice daily with a worn leather bag and a huge and dirty needle, which she plunged into Seamus's buttocks before she waddled to the window, filled the syringe, and screwed syringe into needle.

Three weeks of this and I was desperate for any remedy. The only other medical care on the island, and that most resorted to by the island people, was at the hands of the nuns. So one night Brunella smuggled (for Dr Cuomo was not to know) one of the nuns into the house. 'Pouff,' she said; a little ointment was all that was needed, and a jar emerged from her sleeve. Seamus's lump remained—the charms of Capri receded—I panicked into the arms of the P&O Line and a ship from Naples to Australia. My children never grew up Italian. Nor Seamus a Roman Catholic.

CHAPTER 20

THE SHIP'S doctor, blessedly English, asked to see Seamus for the injection minutes after sailing. 'Is that the patient?' he asked in disbelief as the chubby, rosy cheeked little boy was produced. 'I've never heard such rot.' And that was the last heard of T.B.

On board the ship began the first of Brunella's romances since the unfortunate Forte. It began as the voyage ended— going down the gangway at Sydney Docks. The steward who had waited on her at table pressed a note into her palm as he helped her ashore, and, the first of many, it was brought to me for translation. 'He wants you to go to the cinema tonight.' 'I go,' beamed Brunella. At midnight, she returned, engaged.

Ernie was twenty-one and in Sydney for five days before setting off round the world again. Brunella had four nights off and the promise of a ring on his return. The love letters which Ernie and I, in Brunella's name, wrote to each other did not mention the ring or the impending marriage but were largely Ernie's impressions of foreign ports, foreign girls unfavourably compared to Brunella, and intimations of what he would like to be doing to Brunella. They were pages long. I skipped, in pidgin translation, and then settled, pen in hand, to reply. 'What do you want to say, Brunella?' 'You write, Mrs Dalton. You write nice letter for me.' Brunella's life, or at least that part of it that she could safely relay to Ernie, did not compare with his for eventfulness, so the strain of invention was already becoming too much for me when Brunella finally became bored with the whole process and moved emotionally on.

His name was Roger—improbable, I thought at the time for a Portuguese man, and his English and Brunella's did not have much more in common than had hers with Forte. I dreamed of the days when she would meet a nice Italian boy. The one word on which she seemed to have a firm and rapid grasp was 'engaged'. 'Engaged' in Brunella's vocabulary meant a licence from distant Mama in Capri and ever-present priest around the corner. 'Engaged' meant good intention, both on behalf of Brunella and the current fiancé. A wedding band and a Papal blessing were absent only in question of time—before or after the union, a minor matter. And now, happily settled in Sydney, the need for written communication ceased and I was released from my role of ghost writer. We, my father and I, were not released from the rows. We had all moved in with him and Brunella took on the task of cook-housekeeper to him in addition to that of cook-nanny to the children and myself. In return, we embraced her as one of the family and this meant intimate involvement in her love affairs. Although no letters now had to be written, the space in the flat available for Brunella's privacy was limited, and my father finally rebelled, just as years before he had rebelled in his own married life against a plethora of in-laws, when Roger chased Brunella around the flat, wielding a stick whilst Brunella jumped, shrieking and crying out to God and Mama, over my father's legs, and drowning out both sound and vision of the television set in front of which he was hopefully settled. He put his foot down: Brunella sulked, and I realised that the children had better be packed off to school for at least part of the day. Seamus, just two and a half, had already bitten my father quite firmly on the calf of his leg, and so we thought he might conceivably handle himself with aplomb at school. The headmistress of the kindergarten at Ascham, to which Lisa had gone, consented to take him, albeit reluctantly. Unwisely as well, as it turned out, as his lusty yells were heard from the heights of Darling Point all the way down the hill to the water's edge at Double Bay. They commenced as we turned into the drive and continued until I appeared to retrieve him, and after three days he was expelled. Lisa continued doggedly at Ascham. I became a school mother—the days divided into the time for the taking and fetching of children to and from school—a task which was to continue for years. Two parents can share these tasks. Two parents can share the tales of childish exploits. Two parents can laugh and cry together at childish pranks and childish tragedies. I assumed a double identity—proud mother and stern father. The administrator of spankings and the giver of the healing kiss, never to be allowed the luxury of leaving the room whilst one or the other took place.

I had had the chance of giving them a surrogate father but had rejected it. As well as Brunella, I had had my own shipboard romance, with a startlingly handsome pilot with Middle East Airlines called John Cameron. In the three weeks of our acquaintance and before he left the ship at Fremantle, he had proposed marriage in the most delightful way. 'The more I hear of your circumstances,' he said, 'the more I think you'd better come on my pay-roll as soon as possible.' I had learnt enough to recognise that he was a very nice man. He was visiting his parents who had emigrated to Australia, but he cut short his visit to them in order to come to Sydney to marry me. The hurried preparations I made were, I now realise, undertaken in a daze of unreality. My father, who must have been cast down by the thought of us leaving him again so soon, entered into the spirit of excitement in his customary jovial fashion, and made much of digging out the grey silk top hat bought for my wedding to John Spencer. My close friend Edmee Cameron came up from Tasmania to be whatever attendant seemed appropriate—witness, I expect—and I went off to the local authorities to obtain a licence and make an appointment. We were to be married on a Tuesday by a

Mr Truelove. I still have the licence.

By Tuesday morning, the only items missing were John's divorce certificate, stuck in the post from England, and my resolve. The jokes, the top hat, John's niceness and handsome appeal, my children's precarious financial future, could not blind me to the gut feeling that I was Emmet's wife. His was the name to which I wished to cling and he was the husband to whom I had pledged my life. Death had diminished neither. But John had to get back to Beirut: so, promising to join him soon, I said goodbye, cancelled Mr Truelove and put the top hat back in its box. And I, regretfully, missed the experience of Beirut in its heyday, as I had missed Shanghai. I got on with the business of being a single parent—at Parents' Days, Sports Days, plays, concerts and work shows. My daughter, now a painter, must have then had her eye fixed on distant, more serious horizons for not for her were the bright and painstaking inventions of her friends at the Art Display. At the first end-of-year work table I moved hopefully along listening to the proud murmurs all around me as plasticine models, baskets of fruit, Snow White and the Seven Dwarfs and turreted castles were displayed above the names of my daughter's contemporaries. 'LISA DALTON' I saw looming ahead of me and there, above her name, a solid hunk of plasticine, unshapen and unformed, resting like a cow's droppings on the waiting cardboard. 'GIANT'S HOUSE', proclaimed the label, 'GIANT RESTING INDOORS'. There was no one to share what seemed to me then admirable evidence of contempt for time misspent, or possibly a lofty imagination—no one with

182

whom to ponder if it might be one of these or, perhaps, dare one think of it, evidence of a dull child.

I tried not to bore my friends, and above all not to bore my children with the burden of my solitary thoughts. Mine never asked to be given another father; but, once, after a serious conclave between them, Seamus, aged five, announced that he and his sister had thought hopefully that I might have another baby. 'The only thing is,' he said thoughtfully, 'I'm worried you may not have enough breath left.'

So spoke the future doctor. The Giant's House was perhaps the first stirrings of the future artist.

CHAPTER 21

WHEN WE came back to England, leaving Brunella behind with the latest fiancé, after two years away in Italy and Australia, the house seemed too large, certainly too expensive, and I was still being urged to move by well-meaning friends. Whilst contemplating this, the obvious temporary solution was to look for a lodger. I found him in *The Times* personal column. 'House trained bachelor requires accommodation in sympathetic private house as close to Montagu Square as possible.' He took one look at the large front room which had been Emmet's consulting room now to be converted to become his bed-sitting room, and the small surgery next to it, transformed into a kitchen, ground-floor bathroom, and moved in that day. I hardly saw him, as he left the house each morning around 9 a.m., not, I was to discover later, to go to work but to spend all and every day in Harrods Central Hall. Before he left, a Moyses Stevens florist's van delivered a single red carnation for his buttonhole. He cooked quietly for himself each night, had no visitors, made no noise. I didn't know then that Harrods Hall was a notorious homosexual hunting ground, so I expect he had had his fun for the day.

Slowly we became, if not friends, occasional companions. I was invited in for the odd glass of sherry. I learnt that his last roosting place had been a happy sojourn with another widow, who had lived in Montagu Square and whom he had christened Widow Twankey. I became Twank Two. Just before I sold the house and moved he killed himself but not, for which I was grateful, in my house. Or in Harrods.

* * *

The initial, instantaneous waking dread had subsided: it took about a year to awaken to an unclouded morning; but it happened.

I sold the house reluctantly, and moved to one in Putney. When Emmet died his father had been the first to urge me to move, warning me of impending penury if I continued to live beyond my non-existent means, and suggesting somewhere like Putney. Then I had replied, 'I'd rather go back to Australia', thereby voicing the next worst alternative. Now I'd done one and it had not been all bad it seemed reasonable to try the other.

Whilst the new house was being re-wired and re-roofed and the new owners had moved into mine, we were homeless once more. Chula and Lisba lent me their flat at La Napoule on the Mediterranean coast; the writer Robert Ruark and his wife Ginny lent me their superb apartment in Park Lane. Irish Mary agreed to come to Putney and Swiss and Italian mothers' helps bridged the gaps between Brunella and school.

* * *

We moved into the new house and soon acquired a much more permanent lodger, who was to stay, in a succession of houses, for four years, an Australian friend of my youth whom I'd re-met in Sydney, Hudson Henry.

Hudson, if one could afford him, was a luxury every woman should have in their lives. Kind, generous, attentive, and above all funny, he fulfilled for me the role of major-domo, butler, surrogate father to my children, loving friend and protector, and, if he had lived in another time and place, a court jester. He had gone through one fortune in Australia, had got out just before the tax authorities had caught him, and landed in London on my doorstep to start a job at the *Daily Mirror* selling advertising space—a job I had persuaded the editor, Alex Mackay to give him. Hudson had never sold anything before but threw himself into expense-account luncheons and the city with enthusiasm, selling a record amount of space along the way. I no longer wanted for an escort in London, or a companion on school holidays. The children adored him, the bookmakers adored him, my friends were intrigued by him, and his permanence in our lives only came to an end when he stole the cash from my widowed mother's pension, which was lying on my desk, and tried to blame nine-year-old Seamus. My patience finally snapped. Until then, I had accepted the greengrocer's apologetic accounts rendered for bills I had asked Hudson to pay if I'd been away, the months of unpaid bills at the newsagent, cash similarly spent by Hudson on the horses, even the poor and somewhat simple milkman's tale of how Hudson had managed to extract sixty pounds in cash from him in two dud cheques. I had forgiven the time he came to see me in hospital, recovering from a minor operation, when his debt to me was touching the £6000 mark and his idea of cheering me up was to wheel me to the window in order to admire his gleaming new Jaguar parked outside. I even enjoyed driving around in this splendid prize, the result of one of his rare racecourse wins—Hudson ordering as we turned left, 'Put your arm out, darl: you get six thou' for an arm.'

But the theft of £20 from my pension was the last straw. Hudson left. We did not see each other for a year or two. One night he telephoned, from the airport, en route to Spain where he'd landed a job selling cars. He'd embezzled the splendid expense account, and the *Mirror* had, reluctantly, had to say goodbye.

I asked him where he was, as I heard the pips of the pay phone. 'I'm one step ahead of the posse': he was gone.

I was to see him twice more. Once he came to stay in Menorca where I was renting a holiday home, arriving very late one night, minus a front tooth and with a very drunk, very bewildered French consul in tow, whom he had picked up in a bar in Mahon and persuaded to act as a chauffeur. He'd lost the tooth in another bar in Barcelona when he'd removed it (the real one having been lost years before in a fight) and put it on an adjoining bar stool. The woman who sat on the stool, on discovering a tooth embedded in her bottom demanded the owner. Hudson left without claiming it.

The last time I saw him was in Sydney. He was in hospital, twitching with DTs, his liver destroyed. He clutched my arm and whispered, 'I've left everything to your kids. The family don't know—but my lawyer's got the will.'

He escaped one night from the Home where he was then living, slipped down a rain culvert, broke too many bones, and died. I was back in England when the lawyer contacted me. The will was indeed valid: I was the sole executor, my children sole beneficiaries. The estate was nothing but debts, but as executor I paid for his funeral even to the expensive headstone and lavish flowers ordered by his family, all of them heirs to their mother's fortune.

Once more, bizarre events had intervened to wrap the comforting blanket of laughter around loss. The sting of death has for me more often than not been swabbed with the antiseptic of comedy and, just as death had so often added a touch of melodrama to offset any sorrow in my childhood, so it has managed to invest the remainder of my life with a similar tinge of freakish surprise.

None of us expected Roger Peronnier to leave us sitting gulping down our dry martinis in the Savoy Bar whilst he went upstairs and shot himself. Roger's death would have had nothing like the impact had we not been able to imagine his body upstairs in one of the River suites. The fact that Tam's £400 in notes were in his pocket certainly added to the shock. In the same way, when Blevins Davis, the American friend who had lent us our honeymoon car, died in the lift at Claridge's, the timing was as unfortunate as the event was sad. Blevins had been very rich indeed, but not by birth. He had grown up, alongside his closest friend, Harry Truman, in Independence, Missouri, but fairly late in life had married the heiress to one of the great American railways. Marjorie was a kind and delightful drunk whose own death on one of her own trains left Blevins a wealthy widower. It was reported that she slipped through one of the slats joining the carriages when on her way to the bar—more likely to have been on her way back from the bar. Blevins' generosity thereafter with her money was spectacular and genuine. He was one of the original sponsors of the American Ballet Theatre, the money behind the production of *Porgy and Bess* which toured Europe in the 40s, the dispenser of lavish gifts to friends and charities alike. During the 50s he suddenly and dramatically lost all his money, was declared bankrupt by the US IRS, was forced to sell his magnificent mansion in Independence, his palatial flat in Grosvenor Square, his Rolls Royce in London, and skip to Lima, Peru, where, by some quirk of careless fate, he had bought, forgotten, and failed to declare in his overall estate, an iron ore mine—barren, but in existence. The nine years he subsequently spent, penniless, in Peru were tough ones. We sent each other cards at Christmas but the first I was to hear from him directly was a telephone call from Claridge's in the 1960s. He sounded jubilant.

'Come to lunch. I have exciting news for you,' he said.

It was lovely to see him again, thinner and fitter and full of the stories of his climb back to prosperity. It had taken nine years to find a partner, raise sufficient cash to commence operating the mine, come back to London, and start his life again. He had retained few friends. Most had deserted him. I was one of the few who had not.

'I wanted to tell you that the mine will be worth a fortune and as I have no family I want to see that your children are well provided for. I am going to my lawyer on Monday to make a new will in their favour.' I left Claridge's on air: not only was darling Blevins back in my life but that life began to look immeasurably easier. It was a Saturday. On Sunday at 12.45 the manager of Claridge's telephoned me. Blevins had dropped dead in the lift on his way to lunch. He had blocked the entrance to the lift, and had no doubt given the other guests a nasty turn. The U.S. Ambassador at the time was Walter Annenberg, who showed no sign of displeasure when I telephoned him at home for help. All was done swiftly and expertly for Blevins. He was not, however, able to keep his appointment with his lawyer. And my children were not to grow up rich.

CHAPTER 22

ON OUR return to England from the two years away in Italy and Australia, children at last unprotesting and relatively contained at school for most of the day, time on my hands and precious little money in the bank, I looked around for something to do which would leave me free for the school holiday travels. I had re-met my teenage sweetheart in Sydney, now running a successful advertising agency. We thought it would be a tremendous joke if I did a television commercial for him and it was even more of a joke that the product was a mattress. The mattress was called a Don. On a very hot day in a very small studio, surrounded by an enthusiastic crew, I rolled around on one half of a rumpled double bed on the other side of which was prominently displayed a pipe and a crumpled pillow. I had to look at the camera mouthing in the most sultry tones I could muster 'It MUST be a DON!', while writhing a bit under the sheets. The company won the advertising award of the year. Everyone we knew stayed at home to watch it on the nights it was shown, and it ran for a year.

This gave me the idea that I could perhaps claim experience as a TV performer. Having a few friends in the industry, I telephoned around, and Peter Willes, then Head of Drama at Associated-Rediffusion, put me in touch with a nice woman running their advertising section. Commercial television had just started in competition with the BBC but although they could now produce programmes they had no advertisers as yet to pay for them. In the sparse slots put aside for advertising there were big blank gaps for which nobody was paying. Something called advertising fillers was born and I think I was born to fill them. I soon discovered that, given a microphone, I could talk quite happily until someone pressed a button to stop me. I talked about a variety of things: advice on travelling with young children, for which I was very well qualified; reviewing books for which I was semi qualified if one overlooked training and substituted a certain amount of taste, plus some literary grounding thanks to my grandmother's guidance in childhood; wine tasting for which I believed I was well equipped but not knowing nearly as much as I pretended to know, which was a good deal more, however, than the average viewer in 1960. I must have been quite proficient at it as they got into the habit of telephoning me the night before a slot had to be filled saying, 'Can you fill in two minutes for us tomorrow?'—or five, sometimes ten, sometimes only a minute. This occurred about once a month. Could I regard it as a career? It didn't quite pay the rent but it paid for the odd luxury and encouraged me to feel that an abyss was not about to engulf me. More important, I thoroughly enjoyed it. I forgot about trying to be someone's housekeeper. It did, perhaps, serve as good training.

We were in the swinging sixties: I had grown up and no longer needed to swing. I had joined the working mothers' world. Without a thought or a plan, I then became a literary agent through a set of fortuitous circumstances similar to those which had made me an agent for a foreign government. I was equally ill-equipped and inexperienced but, as with South East Asian politics, I did not get found out until I had had time to learn a little. I also learnt that ignorance coupled with confidence and femininity could prove a positive bonus: men successful in their profession are happy, perhaps flattered, to be asked for help and guidance by a woman. I am not sure that the men who guided me would have been quite so generous with their time to another man. I also believe the role of agent comes more naturally to women, it being more satisfying to nurture than to compete. A healthy proportion of the most successful have been women.

After a fruitful and enjoyable fifteen years as an agent I slid into film producing having spent some years putting together the elements for a film on behalf of my clients. Not many women were producing films then, and the heads of financing studios were nearly all men: bonus time again. Being a woman may not have helped me obtain finance for the five feature films I produced but it gave me the confidence to ask—in two cases, from the most unlikely sources. However, those fifteen years as a literary agent and twenty-five as a film producer are part of another story and do not belong here.

More pertinent here is that, as an agent, I had acquired as a client a successful screenwriter, playwright and novelist, William Fairchild. After twenty-nine fun-filled years of working, travelling and living together, I married him. Unlike many wives of writers, I never felt irritated, thwarted, or neglected by hours he spent at his desk rather than with me, as I derived pleasure and sometimes professional profits from the results. Should he ever ask for my opinion of his work we both knew that our aim was the same. He was prolific, talented and successful enough to need it seldom. He wrote five plays which made it on to the West End stage; some thirty feature screenplays which made it onto the screen; innumerable TV plays; one very good novel and one very amusing non-fiction book. He died before he was able to finish his memoir: that remains, like that of my husband, Emmet's, unfinished and on my conscience as I had promised to finish both. I regret not having done so, if only for the chance of using the title 'Two Hips and a Heart'. This title came from the day I accused him of being a hypochondriac, to which he relied 'Two hips and a heart and I'm a hypochondriac?' He had, indeed, had two hip replacements and a heart operation, following a heart attack.

With this third husband I had, as well as the essential preliminary romance, thirty-seven years of true companionship, laughter, shared interests, and the luxury of a shoulder to lean on. As he called me his 'rock' I think a fair amount of reverse leaning also took place. A great deal of our time together was spent in Biarritz on the south west coast of France where I had bought first an elegant and grand apartment and then a tiny and adorable house on a cliff overlooking a beach. Now after more than forty years it is a second home to me. Bill spent more time there than I could: he could write at his leisure and enjoy being one of the few eligible and attractive men around—for many years he remained legally single. I think the attentions of the eager Biarritz females in which he basked was the reason I finally married him. Those Biarritz years are also part of another story.

After Bill's death, my working years over, the romance-filled years long gone, at ninety-five I still feel the benefits of being a woman: people bring one flowers; accountants are perhaps more patient as one pleads ignorance or incapability; the electrician is more understanding when you tell him you do not know how to insert a light bulb or twiddle a knob on the TV set; the delivery boy shows no sign of irritation when asked to place bags of groceries in specific easy-to-reach corners; neighbours are more lenient when one has grabbed the last parking space. Age may play some part in this, but I think a man would meet with more exasperation. Being a woman has been icing on the cake.

AFTERWORD

I HAD thought of calling these words *Hindsight*, but wondered what age one should reach before a look backwards over one's life becomes either profitable, amusing or instructive.

I had considered *No Hard Shoulder*, which I thought apt. It seemed to me that my event-filled life had taken its various turns, stops and starts, and was propelled thoughtlessly onwards by the fact that there had never been a hard shoulder (the lay by on a motorway) in which to pull in. But this title, *One Leg Over*, is both appropriate and current. I have had much happiness (and my fair share of tragedy, without which it is harder to appreciate the good things) in living a life blessed with love, health and friendship. Contentment is now achieved through two daily experiences. The hot water bottle in bed at night and the hot bath in the morning are privileges for which I thank God, or Providence, vocally. I murmur 'Bliss!' as I hug the waiting bottle. In the morning I say, as I heave myself gingerly up to bath top level, clutching a bar or two and lifting one leg over onto the waiting mat, 'One leg over!'—the day's first and major obstacle accomplished.